Being Human

'Steve Chalke is a brilliant communicator. *Being Human* asks the key questions about life and offers answers which are often funny, always engaging and deeply perceptive. His practical experience of doing what he talks about and his use of excellent illustrations from a wide variety of sources make for a compelling read. This book is too good to miss and will surely make you think about how to become the human being you were meant to be. And, for everyone who recognises that character formation sits at the heart of every healthy education system, this book is gold dust.'

Sir John Rowling, Chairman of PiXL (Partners in Excellence)

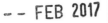

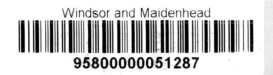

Also by Steve Chalke

The Lost Message of Jesus (with Alan Mann)

Trust: A Radical Manifesto (with Anthony Watkis)

Intelligent Church: A Journey Towards Christ-Centred Community (with Anthony Watkis)

Change Agents: 25 Hard-Learned Lessons in the Art of Getting Things Done

Stop The Traffik: People Shouldn't Be Bought & Sold (with Cherie Blair)

Apprentice: Walking the Way of Christ (with Joanna Wyld)

Different Eyes: The Art of Living Beautifully (with Alan Mann)

Being Human

How to become the person you were meant to be

STEVE CHALKE

HODDER

First published in Great Britain in 2015 by Hodder & Stoughton
An Hachette UK company

This paperback edition first published in 2016.

1

A CIP catalogue record for this title is available from the British Library

ISBN 978 1 444 78947 8
eBook ISBN 978 1 444 78949 2

Typeset in Adobe Garamond Pro by
Palimpsest Book Production Ltd, Falkirk, Stirlingshire

Printed and bound in the UK by Clays Ltd, St Ives plc

Hodder & Stoughton policy is to use papers that are natural, renewable and recyclable products and made from wood grown in sustainable forests. The logging and manufacturing processes are expected to conform to the environmental regulations of the country of origin.

Hodder & Stoughton Ltd
Carmelite House
50 Victoria Embankment
London EC4Y 0DZ

www.hodderfaith.com

Contents

With thanks to the wonderful team which is Oasis both here in the UK and around the world, who constantly help me as I seek to slowly become a better version of myself.

Prologue
The Geese

There is a story told about a flock of tame geese who lived together in a farmyard surrounded by high walls. From time to time they would bemoan their lot in life and complain of boredom, but because the corn was good, and the farmyard was secure, not one of them had ever even unfurled their wings, let alone attempted to fly.

In time a philosopher goose arose from their number. He began to urge them, with great enthusiasm, to give up the mediocrity of their domesticated lifestyle for the joys of free flight. He was very learned and, as they gathered to listen to his wise words, they were impressed by his powerful, motivating arguments and gripped by his eloquent rhetoric.

Week by week he would remind the assembled gaggle that they were birds of flight and would challenge them to fulfil this high calling by taking to the skies. 'My fellow travellers on the way of life, can you, for one moment, imagine that this tiny farmyard, surrounded by its huge walls, is all there is to life for us?' he would cry. 'There is a different story for us; a different destiny. We were born with the gift of wings for a reason. Ask yourself who you are. What kind of goose do you want to become? Discover your true vocation, given to you by your Creator. It is time for us to become the geese that we were always made to be. Let us join our wild cousins in flight.

'Carried by our wings, we could see the world. We too were fashioned to soar above the earth, to lift ourselves beyond the concerns of those who – having no wings – are tied to the ground. Live the life that you were created for. Fly!'

Often the philosopher would reflect on the beauty and wonder of life beyond the farmyard. He would explain to the geese that their forefathers had experienced this outside world as they had stretched their wings to conquer desert wastes and ocean waves, forest glades and mountain ranges. 'But we', he would remind them in solemn tones, 'are imprisoned here in this bland and colourless world. Our wings are folded. Tucked tight into our sides. We are content to paddle in the mud, never even lifting our eyes to the skies that should be our home. What kind of existence is this for a goose? Save yourselves from this wretched waste of a life spent waddling around in the dirt. Become what you were always meant to be. Fly!'

The geese loved the wise old gander's motivational speeches. They found them moving, poetic, inspirational, profound and thought-provoking; a wonderful summary of the meaning and purpose of life. They would honk and squawk their approval as he spoke. And, as they listened, something would stir deep within their breasts, as though a higher power were calling them to the sky. They felt uplifted. Some would even begin to beat their wings to symbolise their commitment to his life-changing message.

More than this, many of the geese gave themselves to constant study of these revolutionary ideas. They devoted themselves to a thoroughgoing analysis and critical evaluation of the great philosopher's teachings and doctrines. They produced learned treatises on the moral, ethical and spiritual implications of flight. They planned academic conferences, held public round-tables and organised seminars, workshops and summer schools to discuss the possible benefits of such a radical breakthrough in lifestyle. They sang anthems to celebrate the gift of flight.

All this they did. But there was one thing they never did. They did not fly! For the corn was good, and the farmyard was secure![1]

The question we have to ask ourselves, as put by the poet Mary Oliver, is what we plan to do with our one wild and precious life.[2]

1 Wake Up!

'I fell asleep in 1992 as a bold, brassy, very confident know-it-all 15-year-old and woke up a 32-year-old single mum living in a council house.'

In 2011 the newspapers reported the story of Naomi – a mother in her early thirties – who was 'thrown back in time' after a rare form of amnesia caused her to forget the past seventeen years.

She woke up believing she was about to sit her school exams in the summer of 1992. But she was stunned to discover she was in fact a mother, with an eleven-year-old son, living in the twenty-first century.

Naomi was told by doctors that she suffered from transient global amnesia – a form of memory loss brought on by stress. 'It wasn't fun . . . I'd fallen asleep in a world of endless possibilities and woken up in a nightmare.'[1]

One of the extraordinary dimensions of this story is, of course, that the contrast between the 'world of endless possibilities' of 'a bold, brassy, very confident know-it-all 15-year-old' and waking up 'in a nightmare' of being a '32-year-old single mum living in a council house' wasn't caused by the amnesia. It was simply highlighted by it.

It's a sobering truth, but without the unusual twist that the transient global amnesia added, Naomi's story – the story of waking up disappointed with life – is the story of millions of people, young and old.

Most of the time, most of us find ourselves immersed in the mundane, preoccupied with getting by, anxious about deadlines; there are bills to pay, emails to write, phone calls to make and trains to catch. We're racing through life but falling asleep on the inside.

However, every now and then – perhaps over a meal or a drink with a friend of many years; or disturbed by a long, sleepless night; or watching the sun set over the sea; or faced with a personal difficulty or family tragedy; or gazing up at the moon and countless stars on a clear summer's night – we momentarily glimpse something bigger, something bolder and more fulfilling.

Our lives are a precious gift. They are sacred; every moment of them. The opportunity to live rather than sleepwalk through our days belongs to us. This book is a call to wake up. It is a call to each one of us; to wake up, to live before we die.

Rabbi Meshulam Zusha, a famous eighteenth-century Polish, Orthodox Jewish leader, told his students, 'In the coming world, they will not ask me: "Why were you not Moses?" They will ask me: "Why were you not Zusha?"'[2]

The journey of life, it turns out, is a quest to find ourselves and our place in the world; a journey of self-discovery.

When I was fourteen I fell in love. I fell in love with a girl called Mary. And, discovering that she went to the local youth club, naturally I joined up too. But after what seemed a lifetime – probably six weeks or so – working as hard as I could to impress her, I was forced to face up to the unthinkable. Mary didn't love me. She was fifteen, I was fourteen. She went to a good school, I didn't. She was beautiful, I was spotty. She was popular, I was awkward. It was never going to work between us. But, even worse than the fact that she didn't want me – I realised she hadn't even noticed me. I was devastated.

Walking home from that youth group in South London on that fateful Friday night, at around 10pm, I found myself faced with a huge decision. Was my life still worth living? I had been rejected by the girl who gave meaning to my future. I know it sounds silly now – but you know how things can be when you are fourteen.

I was wandering up a little street named Dixon Road when it came to me . . .

The youth club happened to be held in a church building, and besides enjoying the table tennis and music, I'd slowly picked up from the people who ran it what it was that inspired them to do so. As far as I could see, their point was this. Every life has value. We are not here by accident. Our existence has intrinsic meaning and purpose. Every person is created by God.

The way I figured it, if this was true, it must include me. So, even if Mary didn't want me, my life was still worthwhile.

This was a very different kind of message to the one that I received, on an almost daily basis, from my school. There the mantra was: 'You are a waste of space. You will never amount to much; you're not intelligent enough. Get used to working with your hands and not your brain. You are not worth educating.'

So it was that on that night, on my way home from that small youth club, I found myself confronted with a choice between two competing stories.[3]

To the school I was nothing more than a statistic – another meaningless life destined to drift along aimlessly until it was eventually swept away on the tide of time with barely a trace left behind. But to the leaders of this youth club, I mattered. My life was significant. In their view, I had been created by a God who claimed to have fashioned me in his image; a God who said that I was here for a purpose.

The choice was mine. But, as far as I was concerned, it was a no-brainer. This new story changed everything. If it were true, my life counted for something. My future mattered. My time was not here to fritter away but to invest. So it was that I decided that even if Mary didn't want me, I'd keep going to that youth club and keep listening hard. And I would tell everyone and anyone I could, from that day on, that life is not barren – we are more than the random by-products of time plus chance – it has purpose.

Beyond that, I also decided that, if all this were true, when I was old enough I would open a hostel – a place of safety for young people who had never been shown that they mattered, to live and thrive and find themselves; a school that taught young people that their lives counted, and a hospital to lavish on them the care that every human deserves, but that so many are denied.

Only this, I decided, was a fitting response to the fact that, on this night, the view I'd gradually gained of myself as an irrelevance had been swept away by the acceptance that my life must have purpose because I was created by God – who, the leaders of the youth club told me, the Bible defines as love.

I say that I decided all this but, at the same time, I felt prompted. Inspired. Guided. Or, to say it as I now understand it: called to serve this God. And though I had little or no understanding of what any of this really meant, I knew it was what I should spend my life doing.

Now, please don't be worried by what I've just said about feeling 'called to serve God'. I'm not trying to go 'religious' on you. In fact, 'religious' was the last thing I have ever wanted to be. Instead, I'd put it like this: until this event I felt I had just been existing, plodding along, getting by. Suddenly, I felt alive.

So, there it was. At the age of fourteen, I had made what I still reckon to be the biggest decision of my life: that I would make the story that I had heard from that youth club the story I would live my life by. No longer would I allow the one that my school offered me determine who I would be, or dominate what I would become.[4] I had woken up – or rather I had been woken up!

A few months ago, I sat chatting, over a cup of coffee, with a senior representative of the British establishment. We talked for a little while about his life. He'd enjoyed the privilege of being educated at one of Britain's most prestigious public schools and then one of its oldest and finest universities. Now, in his mid-forties, he held an extremely influential position professionally. He'd come to see me to discuss a new initiative for which he had been made responsible – developing a national scheme for mentoring young people into excellence.

During our conversation he lamented the number of highly paid, 'professionally successful' people he meets in the course of his work who, he told me, it was clear are simply drifting – sleepwalking – through life.

In response, I told him about the meeting I'd recently been in, in a smart hotel, where I watched a well-known, well-educated public figure slumped, all evening, in a corner by the bar, on his own, drowning in one gin after another. Alone, abandoned and isolated, with a reputation for being socially challenging, he sat there with no one, and nowhere, to go to. His struggle wasn't that he didn't have the right educational qualifications from the right establishments. It was well known that he had the lot. His problem was that his IQ was not matched by his EQ or his SQ[5] – he was intelligent, but emotionally and spiritually illiterate.

The primary question, I suggested, for any mentoring course for young people (or for people of any and every age group) is not about what you do with your life (as important as that question is), but rather, something much deeper: who do you become while you are doing it? It's a question of your character rather than your career.

My visitor looked shocked. He paused before hesitantly explaining that throughout his education and subsequent career he'd never been asked that question. He'd had countless careers advice sessions where he'd been asked about his professional ambitions and his aspirations around salary and lifestyle. But, he said, not once had he ever been confronted with life's primary question: what kind of person do you want to become?

That is what this book is all about. What kind of person do you want to become?

2

Lift that Lid

One of the countries that Oasis – the charity I began in response to my Dixon Road experience – works in is Zimbabwe. As part of our gap-year programme for young school and university leavers, a few years ago a small team spent some months working in Harare, the country's capital city.

It is part of the culture of some of the people groups living in Zimbabwe that the father of a new-born baby will name them after the dominant thought that comes into his head after first seeing his child. That's why female names such as Beautiful, Grace, Lovely, Mercy, Pearl and Pretty are extremely popular.

A year or so beforehand, an Oasis Zimbabwe staff member came across one young girl living homeless and alone on the streets. She'd been given the name 'No Matter' by her father, and had now been abandoned by both of her parents. She came to live with us and get a new start. But because she had no birth certificate or official documentation of any sort, it became the responsibility of our staff to register her with the authorities.

It was the members of our gap-year team who took her to be registered. And, as they queued in the long line with her – lines can be very long in Harare – they slowly formed a plan. Finally, they reached the head of the queue. They stood in front of the official at the desk. 'What's the girl's name?' he asked sternly. Together, with one voice, they replied: 'Precious.'[1]

Much of life, for us all, as I mentioned before, turns out to be a quest to find ourselves and discover our place in the world. Each and every one of us lives in search of a convincing story that explains to us who we are; an overarching narrative that supplies us with a sense of worth and direction; a sense of purpose that wakes us up. 'Find a purpose: the means will follow', the saying goes. Or, to put it in the words of Catholic writer Richard Rohr, 'When you get your, "Who am I?", question right, all of your, "What should I do?" questions tend to take care of themselves.'[2] Without a compelling overarching story – a sense of who we are and of where we fit – we are lost. It's a bit like being shipwrecked, alone, on a desert island; at best we will survive, but we will never thrive.

Hope is a matter of your story, not your mood.

Some of us choose to fill the void left by the absence of such a hopeful story with the pursuit of money, or sex, or power – or perhaps all three. Our hope is that they will bring meaning. But, in truth – even for the few who obtain what they crave

– these pursuits turn out to offer little more than a momentary distraction from life's real quest for the deeper treasures of security, love and a sense of significance. What becomes apparent is that it is far too easy to temporarily, and sometimes tragically, mistake money for security, sex for love and power for significance. And, of course, that is why an indulgence is never satisfying – because we can never get enough of what we didn't want in the first place.

Some of us allow ourselves to become dominated by a story about ourselves that we've inherited from others. We are controlled, even crushed, by its expectations of us, or by the lack of them. We are held captive, rather than set free, by what have become our overarching thoughts and beliefs.

Some of us find ourselves stuck in a rut. It's not that we are living in desperation, but we are not content either. We feel as though we are trapped in a life of second choices; we've not ended up where we would have hoped to be. We don't have the relationship with our family we had wanted. We're not in the marriage we had dreamt of. Our job feels mundane. Life is run of the mill, and we feel imprisoned with no way forward.

One of the most profound truths I have come to recognise over the years is this. In our quest for life, it is not actually death itself that we fear the most. It is, instead, the fear that we might be born, live out our lives, grow old and die, and that none of it will matter. We kick against this feeling of insignificance. It makes us feel very insecure. We feel there must be some meaning to our existence. Our lives can't be meaningless. There must be some epitaph that leaves the message 'I was here'.

However, this sense of angst, unease, of being stuck or of 'lostness', should not be despised. It can be a wonderful gift. The realisation that we are sinking or drifting can bring with it hope and opportunity. This very sense of disorientation, when embraced rather than ignored, can in itself become the impetus that spurs us on to ask deeper questions of ourselves and the world we find ourselves in.

It is an extraordinary fact that if a flea is caught and placed in a jar and the lid is put on, the flea will jump, over and over again, hitting its head on that lid for several days. Any flea is capable of jumping several times higher than the lid of the jar.[3] However, eventually the flea will learn to adapt its behaviour. From that point, whenever the flea jumps, it will always jump just short of the height of the top of the jar. And, surprisingly, when the lid is removed, the flea will still not jump beyond the height of the lid. It has learnt. Its behaviour is set. It has created an imaginary lid for itself which it will never try to break through. It will never attempt to jump beyond the height of the lid again in its lifetime. And, astonishingly, nor will its offspring. The non-existent lid has become the defining factor in their lives, the story that controls their future.[4]

Before Roger Bannister ran the world's first sub-four-minute mile in 1954, the conventional wisdom was that human beings were incapable of running at this speed. Bannister had two major attempts during 1953, but both failed. The popular belief was that the human heart and physique were just not built to take the kind of strain that a sub-four-minute mile would place on them.

But on 6 May 1954, at Oxford University's Iffley Road track, watched by some three thousand spectators, Bannister was about to prove popular opinion wrong. The stadium announcer for the race was Norris McWhirter, who went on to co-publish and become one of the editors of the *Guinness Book of Records*. The crowd cheered Bannister all the way but, though he ran a very fast race and crossed the line first, no one knew whether his effort was good enough to create history. As the minutes crept by they fell uncannily silent. Then, finally, came McWhirter's announcement:

Ladies and gentlemen, here is the result of event 9, the one mile: 1st, No. 41, R. G. Bannister, Amateur Athletic Association and formerly of Exeter and Merton Colleges, Oxford, with a time which is a new meeting and track record, and which – subject to ratification – will be a new English Native, British National, All-Comers, European, British Empire and World Record. The time was 3 . . .

The roar of the crowd was instant, and drowned out the rest of the announcement. Bannister's time was 3 minutes 59.4 seconds.

But, just forty-six days later, on 21 June, Bannister's world record was broken by his rival John Landy, an Australian athlete, who ran a time of 3 minutes 57.9 seconds. Within a year, thirty-seven other runners had done it, and within three years another 300!

It is amazing what can be achieved once the imaginary lid has been lifted.

Our greatest danger in life is not that we aim too high and miss, but that we aim too low and hit our target.

So, how do we come to own a story bold enough to motivate and guide us? How do we come to own a story big enough to remove our imaginary lid?

3

The Big Story

'Our chief want is someone who will inspire us to be what we know we could be,' wrote Ralph Waldo Emerson, the great American poet.

Those words capture perfectly my experience on that Friday night in 1969, in South London. I remember the whole thing like it was yesterday. Suddenly my life was not just, or even primarily, about 'my story' any more, but rather about '*the* story'. I felt as though I was lifted out of the pettiness that had consumed so much of my energy to that point, and into a different dimension. As a result I've slowly come to understand life in a particular way, which has brought shape, meaning and hope to my journey thus far. My small, flawed, personal micro-story was given a bigger, global, even cosmic context as it was caught up into God's big story.

Now, let's get things straight from the start. You know I asked you not to get worried about all that religious stuff? Well, what I meant was this.

That Friday night in London, I chose to become a 'follower of Jesus'. I use that term deliberately, rather than the more generic 'Christian' for now, simply because, unfortunately, it has become overloaded with – if not buried beneath – centuries of cultural baggage and negative associations.

Following Jesus isn't about signing up to endless outdated or repressive religious doctrines and theories. Indeed, for anyone who is tempted to get religiosity confused with faith, it is perhaps helpful to remember that it was organised religion – the rigid teachings, opinions, doctrines and creeds of the priests of his day – that killed Jesus.

Making the story of Jesus the story that you live by doesn't mean adopting an anti-intellectual and overly literalistic view of the Bible's text and insisting that the world was made in six days, just over six thousand years ago. It doesn't mean believing that the world is going to end soon, or even wishing that the world would end soon. It doesn't mean preferring death to life, faith to reason, or censorship to debate. It doesn't mean becoming dogmatic or savagely judgemental or thinking that everyone who disagrees with you is going to burn in the abyss forever. Nor does it mean opposing human rights, women's rights, gay rights, individual moral autonomy, freedom, remarriage, stem cell research, the use of condoms, innovation, other faiths, atheists, sex, fashion, the teaching of evolutionary biology, the big bang or particle physics.[1]

What it does mean is giving your life to the story that at the very heart of the universe is a God of love who is on the side of all those who are oppressed and forgotten, who feel insignificant and powerless, and who calls us to join in the revolutionary movement to bring hope and real liberation to all.

This, I discovered, is the story revealed through Jesus' life and example. And this is the story which has brought direction to my life and that breathes into Oasis its sense of ongoing purpose. This is the story which not only shapes all our work but continues to inspire and inform our future vision.

Several years ago I had the joy of visiting Rio de Janeiro for a few days. I was there to work but had an afternoon free and was determined to visit the iconic *Christ the Redeemer* statue that sits atop Corcovado mountain overlooking the city. As I climbed the steep steps that led up the mountain my excitement grew, but then, in an instant, it was dashed as I came face to face with a blocked gate and a sign which, in English, read: '*Christ the Redeemer*. Out of Order. Service will be restored as soon as possible.' I've never forgotten what seemed to me to be, though unintentional, a deeply profound statement.

From the picture of Jesus that is presented by sections of our media, not to mention the Church, it is perhaps all too easy to reach the conclusion that the Christian story is broken. But the way I see it, the teaching of Jesus is, instead, like a fabulous but long-buried treasure, encrusted in debris, tarnished and discoloured by neglect, half buried in mud and muck that has slowly engulfed it over two thousand years. But clean away the dirt and encrustations, and what you are holding is beautiful. It is priceless. As Jesus put it, I've come to show you how to live a life that's worth living.[2]

Throughout the 1990s I had the privilege of working in my spare time, as Oasis developed, as a television presenter. It was a wonderful and enriching experience that changed the way I thought forever. I'd grown up in a form of Christianity that was convinced it was right about everything. That the truth – the whole truth and nothing but the truth – had been revealed to us, and that even other forms of the Church were in differing degrees of error. More than that, the rest of 'the world' was filled with people living morally reprobate lives in defiance of God. Mixing with them could seriously damage my moral and spiritual health. I was to discover that the opposite was true!

In fact, when I first got a job in TV, one of the leaders of my denomination wrote to me to express his concern and warn me about all this – especially about the women who, he thought, might ensnare me.

The reality was different. I met loads of wonderful people – men and women – who loved life but, like me, sometimes struggled with it. They were lots of fun to work with. They were hardworking and kind. They could be very generous, though, once again, just like me, they sometimes acted selfishly. They were good people. They were open, honest and vulnerable, I loved them, and we had some extraordinary conversations: 'I'm not religious or anything like that, but . . .' and, with that, off we would set on another deep and rambling conversation about life, its richness and its meaning. 'I'm not a church-goer, but we're getting married and we want it to be about something more than a legal agreement; would you pray for us at our wedding?' 'I wouldn't call myself a Christian, but I want to thank God for our new baby. Would you do a blessing?' 'My marriage has broken down. Will you say a prayer for me? Can we talk?'

Here is the wonderful thing. As we talked about these things, all these people told me how much I had helped them. But the truth is, they did far more for me than I ever could for them. They opened my eyes.

What none of them believed was that attending church services would add anything of value to their lives; they didn't see any possibility of it offering them any sort of vision of God and human existence that was inspiring or useful, or providing them with any skills or resources for coping more effectively with the humdrum of day-to-day life. In fact, in their minds, church was for self-righteous religious fanatics – the God Squad! What they were searching for wasn't doctrine or dogma, but meaning and life.

But every one of them had faith.

Which got me thinking. Perhaps it would be a huge help to us all if we stopped using phrases like 'I am a Christian' or 'I'm not a Christian' all together and, instead, concentrate on how we can behave in 'Christian' or 'Christ-like' ways. Why would this help us? Because then we would begin to see Christian faith as a 'practice', a set of habits and behaviours modelled by Jesus, and designed to set us free to live, rather than a repressive belief system.

A well-known religious leader found himself introduced to a young woman who had only recently joined a church community. 'Are you a Christian?' he wanted to know. She looked shocked. 'Only my friends can answer that one,' she said.

Jesus never wrote a set of doctrines, he never started a denomination and, I put it to you, never intended to begin a new religion. He simply demonstrated a different way of living – loving God and loving others the way we love ourselves – and invited others to 'follow him' in that.

I am fascinated by Jesus. The quest of my life has simply been to understand him – what he said and did, how he lived, why he died and what his resurrection means. And, almost half a century after I first began to follow him, although I have learnt much from other teachers and philosophies, what he said and did makes more sense than anything I have heard anywhere else.

It turns out that originally the followers of Jesus were simply known as 'people of the way'; people who identified with the way of life Jesus taught and demonstrated. The term 'Christian' only appears three times in the entire Bible, was never used by Jesus[3] and was originally coined as a way of ridiculing Christ's followers; invented by their opponents, a decade or so after Jesus' death, to mock the 'people of the way'. The problem is that not only has it stuck, it has somehow been transformed into a badge of honour!

Jesus was, of course, born and bred a Jew, and he never seems to have shown any desire to abandon the faith of his fathers. Rather than a religion, however, Judaism was seen as a 'way of life' in which people chose to walk.[4] That's why the famous Old Testament writer Isaiah made the claim: 'This is the way; walk in it.'[5]

In this context, Jesus' famous words, '*I am* the way, the truth and the life',[6] take on an extraordinarily dynamic and subversive edge, Following Jesus, it turns out, isn't about religion and all its paraphernalia; it is simply about a way of walking the road of life.

Which is why, of course, the early followers of Jesus designated their faith as 'The Way'.[7] Following Jesus was a revolutionary way of doing life then – it still is today. It is about placing faith in him. It is not about attending church services, singing hymns, playing the guitar and listening to sermons, without any of them necessarily making a scrap of difference to the way we are and the way we live. Following Jesus is not about belief – in the sense of assent to a system of doctrinal statements. Real faith is about trusting Christ enough to walk his way through life; it's about letting his story shape our actions, our attitudes, our responses and initiatives.

Faith is a funny thing. It gets ridiculed by some as escapism, avoidance and delusion, while those who claim it for themselves are dismissed as misguided, deceived, brainwashed and even mad. The strange thing is, however, in my experience it's faith that demands we dispense with illusion and face reality. The culture of contemporary 'common sense' seems unable to serve up anything beyond a constant diet of denial about life; fluffy pretending, shallow excitement and trivial entertainment. And its speciality is the daydream of success untinged by failure, disappointment, mundaneness and mortality.

What's more, there is a widespread myth that somehow faith is the exclusive possession of those who hold religious beliefs. This is false. The real question, then, is not 'Do you have faith?' Rather it is, 'Are the people, the organisations, the investments, the ideas, the promises, the dreams and the relationships you put your faith in day by day, year by year, really worth your investment of trust?'

The difference, for instance, between believing that God exists and believing that God does *not* exist is not the difference between the 'presence' and 'absence' of faith – it is simply a difference in the *content* of that faith and belief.

While we are on the subject of God, some theologians and philosophers refer to God as 'the ultimate source', 'the ground of being', 'the prime cause' as well as other perfectly logical but equally impersonal terms. Traditionally, church people (along with our Jewish and Muslim cousins) have talked primarily about God as a father, and sometimes as a mother,[8] a safe fortress, a good shepherd, a rock, a shield, a guiding light and many others. For the record, although throughout this book I will usually refer to God as 'he' or 'him', two truths must be recognised. First, God always remains far greater and more inclusive than any of our images. Second, because of our personal experience of life, we are almost bound to find some of these pictures more helpful than others.

What the Bible never describes God as, though, is a magician.

'If only God would give me some clear sign! Like making a deposit in my name in a Swiss bank account,' once said Woody Allen. There are times when we would all love God to intervene miraculously and transform our circumstances – and, of course, occasionally we witness or hear about this happening. Far more commonly however, we experience God as a faithful, supportive presence to help us cope with the successes and the disappointments, the hopes and the fears, the curiosity and the boredom, the bewilderment and the irritation, the despair and the exhaustion, the pain and the pleasure of life.

My experience is that God is a constant presence, of whom I am sometimes aware and yet, all too often, fast asleep to. And so, I've learnt that I don't need to ask God to be present: God is always present, which means that I don't need to go looking for him in a church building, or a mosque, or a synagogue, or a cathedral, or a temple, or a shrine, or in a garden, or up a mountain, or on a beach – although, at times, one or more of these might prove to be of great help to me.[9]

Jesus summed it up in the brilliant short story he told about a wise man who built his house on rock and a foolish man who built his house – no doubt with a lot less effort and cost – on sand. He was trying to get people to think about who they were and where they were going in life; about who they wanted to become.

'Follow me,' he said.[10]

4

Punching Holes

As a small boy Robert Louis Stevenson, the famous nineteenth-century Scottish novelist, would sit gazing out of the window of his parents' home, watching the evening shadows fade and dusk give way to darkness. He was fascinated by the old-fashioned lamplighter, who each night would wander down the street lighting the gas street lamps one by one. It is said that on one occasion he was so excited by this that he shouted to his nanny, 'Look, there's a man coming down the street punching holes in the darkness!'[1]

That's our job – our mission, should we choose to accept it – to punch holes in the darkness of poverty, of prejudice, of injustice, of loneliness, of intolerance, of rejection and of hatred; to follow Christ and work with God as agents of change.

The most famous prayer that Jesus taught those who choose to follow him begins with the words:

Our Father in heaven,
hallowed be your name,
your kingdom come,
your will be done
on earth as it is in heaven.[2]

I've slowly learnt that to pray a prayer that big is to do more than say some words. To really pray any prayer is to allow its content to become your vision, your passion, your longing, your commitment. To pray Jesus' prayer is to allow it to shape you; to become the story by which you choose to live your whole life. As Søren Kierkegaard observed, 'The function of prayer is not to influence God, but rather to change the nature of the one who prays.'

So, what is the 'kingdom of God', or the 'kingdom of heaven'[3] as it is sometimes called in the Bible? There's a joke about the fact that what Jesus spent most of his time teaching about was the kingdom of God, but what he got was the Church! It is based on the fact that although Jesus only ever used the word 'church' on two occasions, he talked about the 'kingdom of God' or 'kingdom of heaven' all the time, every day, almost every hour. He seems to have had a bit of a one-track mind![4]

I've realised that Jesus' prayer is really an invitation to me – to you – to all of us – to follow him in the way we live, thus joining in with the unfolding story of the establishing of the 'kingdom of God', which is simply another way of talking about what life would be like if God were king; if *his* will was done here on earth, rather than that of the financiers, the markets and the politicians. And, as the rest of Jesus' life, teaching and example makes plain, the will of God is simply this: that every person, every community, indeed the whole of creation, should flourish, free from oppression, and enjoy living well.

The kingdom of God is a way of doing things; a way of doing things differently. The excluded are welcomed, the hungry are fed, difference is celebrated rather than scorned, injustice is banished, greed is no more, no one is oppressed or abused, disease is eradicated, joy and fulfilment become a reality rather than a distant dream.

There's an ancient term, widely used by writers of Celtic spirituality. It talks of 'thin places'; places where the gap between earth and heaven is said to be very narrow; places where you can sense God more strongly than in the mundane monotony of everyday life. The Celts taught that, even ordinarily, heaven and earth are only a few feet apart but that, in a thin place, the gap is even smaller. It's not just thin places, however. There are 'thin moments', 'thin experiences' and 'thin people', where the porous threshold between the two realities becomes more so.

The adventure of life, for me, from that night in South London to this very moment, continues to be that of playing my small part in God's transformation and renewal of the whole earth by working to create thin places and thin moments where hope and well-being can leak into local communities as well as into the lives of individuals.

But here's the thing. Many people make a false assumption. They conclude that because one of Jesus' aims was to teach people how to live well, we need to look elsewhere – almost anywhere else – for answers to the question of how to have fun! Deep down we are convinced that any and all teaching about behaviour is designed to stop us from being happy or fulfilled. The premise of this book, however, is simply that the more we really come to understand these two goals – to live ethically and to live happily – the more we are able to see that, far from pulling us in different directions, they belong together. The way Jesus himself put it was that when we seek God's kingdom and his justice as a priority, everything else begins to fall into place.[5]

Others make a different mistake. They assume that the story of the Bible – understood best through the lens of the life and message of Jesus – is primarily, even exclusively, centred around God's forgiveness of our sins and failings. The truth, it seems to me, is even more unexpected and generous than all this. The overarching story of the Bible is that the God of the universe is working to establish his kingdom of love, justice, inclusion and peace, here on earth, where he calls as many of us who will, to be his partners – his agents – and to work with him in the great task of the transformation of our world.

By the way, though 'sin' is a kind of 'uncool' word that's out of fashion – except with the tabloid press, who misuse it grossly – it is actually just a shorthand way of talking about everything that de-humanises us; that messes us up; that reduces us and others, including our shortcomings, screw ups and general self-centredness. Jesus, on the other hand, came to show us how to be more human – to live at peace, both internally and externally.

It is clear from the reality of life around us, and from Jesus' own words, that the kingdom of God is, at one and the same time, both already present and still a longed-for future hope. While teaching his followers to pray and work for the transformation of the world, Jesus also explained, 'The kingdom of God is in your midst.'[6] Although through Jesus' life and work God's kingdom was already beginning to break in, its ultimate fulfilment is still in the future.[7]

This 'now and not-yet-ness' of the kingdom of God is what William Booth, the founder of the Salvation Army, was speaking about when he ended his last-ever public address, in London's Royal Albert Hall, on 9 May 1912, with the words:

> While women weep, as they do now, I'll fight; while little children go hungry, as they do now, I'll fight; while men go to prison, in and out, in and out, as they do now, I'll fight; while there is a drunkard left, while there is a poor lost girl upon the streets, while there remains one dark soul without the light of God, I'll fight.

The 'now and not-yet-ness' of the kingdom of God is what we wrestle with each day of our lives. People often ask, 'If God has the power to sort all of the world's woes, why doesn't he?' 'If God is all-powerful and pure love, if God is in control, then why doesn't he act?'

Does God look down on the poverty and oppression of billions and, although he hears their prayers and petitions, choose to turn his back? Does he listen to the desperate cry of the dispossessed, the forgotten, the abused, the oppressed and betrayed, and simply ignore or reject their plea?

No. God is not holding out on us. God is love, as an early follower of Jesus defines him in the Bible.[8] God is on our side. The problem is that God does not always get what God wants. Which is part of what Jesus was referring to when he taught us to pray, 'Our Father in heaven . . . your kingdom come, your will be done on earth as it is in heaven', rather than calling us to recite a prayer of thanksgiving that all was well. And it's why he calls us to follow him in working as agents of change and transformation.

This thought, that God doesn't always get what he wants, upsets many religious people – they claim that if God is all-powerful, he can do anything he wants and that to suggest otherwise is an affront to him.[9] But here is the truth. I know that God doesn't always get his way. I am absolutely certain of it. Why? If nothing else, simply because of the way I behave. I, like all other human beings, have been given the freedom to do my will and, to my regret, it doesn't always coincide with God's will.[10]

Traditionally Christianity, along with the other two Abrahamic religions (Judaism and Islam), has attributed omnipotence – unlimited power and control – to God. The way I see it, however, not only does this view not marry up with the reality of the world as we encounter it, it doesn't fit with the message of the Bible either.

We live in a world where God's will is clearly not done 'as it is in heaven'. Paul of Tarsus, an ancient city which is now in modern-day Turkey, was the famous follower of Jesus who gave his life to bring the revolutionary story of Jesus and the kingdom of God to people around the Roman world. When he writes to his friends in the city of Ephesus, Paul, who understands this ongoing 'struggle', explains that it is 'not against flesh and blood, but against the rulers, against the authorities, against the powers of this dark world' as well as 'against the spiritual forces of evil in the heavenly realms'.[11]

The question is, what did Paul mean? It is clear. He speaks both of human rulers and authorities and then of the spiritual forces of evil that lie behind them. According to him, governments, regimes, traditions, institutions and corporations can all develop organisational values, structures and cultures that are malevolent. But, beyond the will of their leaders and members, there is often a systemic oppressive spirituality, bigger and more powerful than any of the individuals involved, which grips and possesses them. Paul is challenging us to take the socio-political nature of evil seriously without ever minimising its individual and personal aspects. We are to fight systematic evil as forcefully as we are to fight individual wrongdoing.

Beyond even this, however, there are events and problems that cannot be attributed, in any direct sense, to the moral choices of humans or our political, economic and cultural structures:

a painful death resulting from an incurable terminal disease, the suffering caused by earthquakes, hurricanes, floods, volcanic eruptions, forest fires, droughts and tsunamis. It is interesting that these catastrophic events are frequently referred to by insurance companies as 'acts of God', simply because of the belief that if the blame for them cannot be laid at humanity's door, God must be culpable!

But, as C. S. Lewis puts it in his classic book *Mere Christianity*: 'Enemy-occupied territory – that is what this world is. Christianity is the story of how the rightful king has landed, you might say landed in disguise, and is calling us all to take part in a great campaign of sabotage.'

The message of Jesus was never an evacuation plan designed to offer us an escape from reality. Rather, it's a transformation plan for our broken and conflicted world. Empowered by God's Spirit, we are called to serve as his active moral agents as we work to bring about the will (the kingship or kingdom) of God 'on earth as it is in heaven'.[12] Jesus' prime intention in calling us to follow him, to walk his way, was not to prepare us for the next life, but to help us experience heaven's life here and now, in the ordinariness of our everyday existence.

God doesn't always get what he wants, but the curve of history is bending towards justice. The promise will eventually be fulfilled. This is what Charles Jennens was referring to when in 1741 he sent his friend George Handel the lyrics he had penned for what was destined to become the now world famous 'Hallelujah Chorus', as part of a new oratorio *The Messiah*:[13]

The kingdom of this world;
is become
the kingdom of our Lord,
and of His Christ,
and of His Christ.
And He shall reign for ever and ever.
Hallelujah, hallelujah, hallelujah, hallelujah.

God's great story is more than a story to read. It's a story that gives humanity direction and purpose. Each one of us is invited to be part of God's great drama – to become players in the task of bringing his will to the earth.

Our mission – should we choose to accept it – is to work with God, as agents of change, to punch holes in the darkness. To live deliberately. To create thin places, thin moments – to be thin people until his kingdom, his kingship, comes to our world in its completeness.

Ivan Illich, the Austrian philosopher and Roman Catholic priest, explained it like this:

> Neither revolution nor reformation can ultimately change a society, rather you must tell a new powerful tale, one so persuasive that it sweeps away the old myths and becomes the preferred story, one so inclusive that it gathers all the bits of our past and our present into a coherent whole, one that even shines some light into the future so that we can take the next step forward. If you want to change a society, then you have to tell an alternative story.[14]

The Bible has hundreds of stories – many of which have become well known around the world – but it only has one big story, one central theme. And it's a story worth being part of!

5
Seeing is Believing

Aristotle, an ancient Greek philosopher who lived 350 years before Jesus, taught that there are three important steps to becoming the person you were meant to be.

First, he said, it is important to aim at the right goal in life – for which he used the Greek word *telos*,[1] meaning 'end' or 'ultimate purpose'.

We are familiar with the word *telos* because of our use of another Greek word, *tele*, which comes from the same root, meaning 'far away' or 'distant', and is used in English words such as telephone, telescope, television and telegraph. Our objective in life, according to Aristotle, is to focus on this distant or ultimate goal. Only in the light of this can we live well today. He then explained that this ultimate purpose is determined by the story – complete with the beliefs and values it promotes – that we choose to live within.[2] It is this vision that, in the end, not only forms but directs our worldview, expectations and aspirations.

Next, Aristotle suggested that each of us needs to work out which strengths of character – or virtues as he called them[3] – we need to develop in order to become the kind of person who is equipped to achieve our *telos* or ultimate goal.

Finally, he explained, we need to master habits that support our chosen virtues by working to make them a matter of instinct or second nature.[4]

Aristotle taught that the *telos* of life was *eudaimōnia*, a Greek word which is often translated as 'happiness', though perhaps a little more accurately as 'human flourishing', 'the good life' or 'well-being'. *Eudaimōnia*, however, he said, should not be confused with an emotion – which comes and goes – but is rather a state of ongoing well-being that is enjoyed by those who live virtuously by cultivating the right habits.

Our vision of life is determined by what we consider happiness or well-being to look like: a life of pleasure, a big family, money, professional success, power, strong and lasting friendships, the perfect partner, celebrity, time to ourselves, the service of others? The answers are numerous.

If your life was a story, what would it be about? What would be its most important themes? What would its *telos* be? And what virtues and habits would you need to develop to achieve it?

'Gotta Serve Somebody', a song written by Bob Dylan,[5] won the Grammy Award for Best Male Rock Vocal

Performance in 1979. In it, Dylan paints a picture of people from a huge variety of walks of life: millionaires, hairdressers, builders, socialites, preachers, doctors, warlords, sports champions . . . all with one thing in common. The oft-repeated chorus drives home the song's theme and title: 'You're gonna have to serve somebody'. I was in my early twenties when the song was released. Its lyrics made a huge impression on me.

John Lennon, however, was unimpressed. In his diary he wrote: 'The backing was mediocre . . . the singing was really pathetic, and the words were just embarrassing.' And, in response, he composed and recorded his own song, parodying Dylan's lyrics, called 'Serve Yourself'![6]

We tend to assume that it was more primitive peoples that served gods. For instance, the gods and goddesses of the Greeks: Zeus the god of fate; Ares of war; Aphrodite of love, pleasure and beauty; Eros of sexual desire; and Hades, the lord of death and the afterlife. Whereas, in our enlightened times, we've been set free from all that kind of thing.

In truth, there are as many gods on display in our society – all vying for our adoration – as in any that went before us. Their names might have changed, we are more direct now – money, sex, power, the market, leisure, or self-interest, health and beauty – but their characters have remained stubbornly the same.[7] And, as has often been remarked, in the end we never possess our desires; instead they possess us and we serve them.

'We are money chasers. It is the only game in town. We are obsessed. We see nothing else but money,' claimed Muhammad Yunus, the Nobel Peace Prize-winning Bangladeshi economist, in a radio interview for the BBC in 2012.

> But human beings are not money-making robots. Money making is a means, but somehow it has become a means and an end. We forgot that, as if money making is the only thing we are supposed to do; as if money making is the only thing we can do. This is a minor part of our life. What is the purpose of our life on this planet? Our real purpose is to contribute to the planet so that it is a safer and happier place to live.[8]

Human beings are decision-making beings. We all make choices. We all choose who, or what, we will serve, but we have an insatiable desire to worship someone or something. 'You can take away a man's gods,' claimed the famous psychologist Carl Jung, 'but only to give him others in return.' You've got to serve somebody or something – even if it is only yourself.[9]

If our lives are a story, the question is: what is the ultimate goal of that story? Once that *telos* is recognised and 'owned', it becomes much clearer which values, habits, practices and attitudes we should, and shouldn't, adopt and develop in order to get there.[10] Discovering your story delivers you a wake-up call. It brings you to life.

The story is told of how Sir Christopher Wren, the great British architect, was out evaluating progress on the building of

London's new St Paul's Cathedral. He had designed it as a replacement for the previous cathedral, destroyed by the Great Fire three years earlier in September 1666. Unrecognised by the workforce he wandered around the site chatting casually to some of the craftsmen. He stopped and asked a stonecutter what he was doing. 'I am cutting stone to earn myself a living,' was the reply. Pondering this slightly disappointing response, Wren walked a little way further before stopping again to ask another stonecutter the same question. 'I am helping Sir Christopher Wren build a magnificent cathedral that will stand for centuries to come in honour of God.'

Our perception of what we are doing – earning a living or leaving a legacy – not only determines our approach to our work but, even more fundamentally than that, it shapes what we spend our time thinking about, and therefore learning and becoming, in the process of doing our work.

Every one of us lives in a story of some sort, an overarching framework that determines our attitude to ourselves, our relationships, our possessions, our fears and frustrations, our hopes and aspirations and, even more critically, what we are learning as we live. Life is not static – we are creatures in continuous development!

Every human has an innate need for story in their life. We are like sponges. We soak up insight and understanding about who we are, and therefore how to behave, from the world all around us. This means that the question is never 'Are we being influenced?' but rather 'What, or who, are we being influenced by?'

What are the assumptions that we are making about our lives and behaviour without even being aware that we are doing so? What are the 'norms' that we have come to take for granted that are shaping and releasing us, or limiting and boxing us in?

I sometimes wear sunglasses – they help me see in certain conditions, but they also colour the way I see everything I am looking at. However, because I can take them off, I can get to understand how they are adding to, or detracting from, my view of the world around me.

The problem is that we all wear 'cultural sunglasses'. We all have a worldview – the lenses through which we see the world – which is shaped by the culture into which we were born, our upbringing, our education, our friends and relationships, our job, our successes and failures, and all sorts of other factors. This worldview (our way of seeing, understanding and explaining the world) helps or hinders us in determining our responses to life's big questions.[11]

The reason that all this is difficult is that, because we wear these cultural spectacles behind our eyes rather than in front of them, it's impossible to take them off to analyse the way in which they colour and filter our view of things – not just what we see of the world, but what they make us blind to. And, perhaps most alarmingly, for many people these lenses are worn unconsciously, which is what makes them so fascinating and, at the same time, why they can be so dangerous.

Take a simple example: the impact that culture – our way of seeing things – has on our view of beauty. What makes a person attractive? What constitutes a 'compliment', and what form should it take? In some cultures, telling a woman she is putting on weight is praise indeed, while in many others exactly the opposite is true!

Or eye contact. In Western culture, deliberate lack of eye contact in a conversation can indicate a number of underlying issues, but they are all decidedly negative – lack of interest, rejection, embarrassment, depression, a sense of inferiority or even outright fear. In China, however, lack of eye contact may indicate great respect, whereas in many Muslim countries, a woman may seek to evade eye contact with a man in order to avoid sexual impropriety. And among the North American Navaho people it may be an attempt to escape soul theft.

Then there is food. The world is filled with conflicting cultural assumptions around food. How to serve it, how to be seated around it, which utensils are appropriate to use to eat it, how to request it, refuse it, or thank your host for it.

For some years, one of the world's best-known banks ran an advertising campaign around the challenge presented by this diversity of international cultural perceptions. Perhaps the most memorable television ad was of an English businessman who was visiting a restaurant in China with his hosts.

On the menu is eel soup. The Englishman hates eel soup. And, to make matters worse, the eels are fresh and killed at the table. But, because the man doesn't know much about Chinese food customs, even though he can hardly bring himself to look at what he is eating, he forces himself to finish all that is in his bowl, only to find that he is served an even bigger eel in an even larger dish. Determined to be polite, whatever the personal cost, for fear of losing the important deal that he is in China to secure, he manages to finish this off as well, only to discover that, as a reward, he is now brought another giant eel to tuck into.

The commentary to the film makes this observation:

> The English believe it's a slur on your host's food if you don't clear your plate.
>
> Whereas the Chinese feel you are questioning their generosity if you do.
>
> Never underestimate the importance of local knowledge.[12]

Never underestimate the power of the story you live in to shape how you look at things, as well as to determine the way that you behave.

A few years ago I went through a period in my life where I was doing so much travelling that I would regularly forget where I was. It sounds slightly ridiculous but I'd wake up in the morning to the sound of my alarm at an unearthly hour and, before I opened my eyes, try to remember my location: at home or in a hotel, in the UK or elsewhere in the world? Then, having worked out the answer, I'd pose myself a second, associated, question: 'What am I here for?'

I remember the alarm going off very early one morning when I just couldn't get my bearings at all. Even when I opened my eyes I was still in the dark, both literally and metaphorically. It wasn't until I pulled back my hotel-room curtains that I remembered I was in Manhattan, New York, having flown in from Chicago very late the night before. Only then did I recall what I was there for – a business meeting. The point is this. Once I had focused where I was and why I was there, I knew how to dress – a suit – and how to prepare for the day ahead. If, when I'd opened those curtains, it had revealed that I was on a Mediterranean beach I would have behaved and dressed very differently.

In the end, for us all, the way we behave is determined by the story we find ourselves in. A person becomes what they believe.

So, the thing is that it's only in the light of being clear about our story that we can really begin to think consistently. It is only in response to our *telos* – our ultimate goal – that we can begin to sort out what we believe about issues as fundamental as relationships, money, credit, music, politics, the environment, fashion, war, sex and sexuality, careers, guns, animal rights, food, drugs, art, transport, family, gender, democracy, military intervention, sport, business, religion, community, education, healthcare, poverty, employment, immigration, leadership, truth, worship, friendship, priorities, work, volunteering, success, failure, forgiveness, punishment, crime, disability, race, colour, parenting, priorities, honesty and, of course, the meaning of life itself.

Even in the 'little' decisions it's only our big story, with its sense of ultimate purpose, which is capable of steering us reliably. Only it is powerful enough to supply us with the focus we need.

How, for example, do you decide whether to go out with your friend, who has just called you to say that they would like to see you tonight, or to stay in and prepare for tomorrow's meeting? It is impossible to make the wisest choice based on rules such as 'I always stay in midweek' or 'I always put my friends before my work' or, on the other hand, 'work before friendship every time'. Only the story you live in – that you have chosen, or allowed to become yours – can guide you. Which decision – to go out or to stay in – is more important to the story of your life and its *telos*? You can only make these choices – which are all moral decisions – in the light of your overarching goal.

'Seeing', they say, 'is believing'. The story you live in becomes the lens through which you see the whole of life. Which means that becoming the person you were meant to be is, first and foremost, about the story you choose to be part of!

6 Rekindling Imagination

'Imagination is more important than knowledge', said Albert Einstein.

If the greatest barrier to achievement is the inability to see, it's our imagination that sets us free, or boxes us in. Remember those fleas in that jar? The baggage of our past experience all too easily becomes our controlling story. It blurs and distorts our view of ourselves and reality, and so continues to shape, determine and often limit our future. And when that happens, our sense of *telos* or direction and destination can sometimes be lost all together.

I was more than a little intimidated as I walked into the recreation hall of one of Britain's 'Category A' prisons. I had been invited to speak to several hundred men whose freedom had been removed from them for good reason. These high-security institutions are reserved for convicts whose escape would be very dangerous for the public or for national security. They are filled with murderers, rapists and the perpetrators of other violent crimes.

One of the guards led me to the stage. I perched on the stool that had been provided, tried to look as relaxed as possible and began talking. However, I soon discovered that those who had gathered to listen to me were one of the most appreciative audiences I had encountered for some time.

For the next thirty minutes or so I chatted about life, hope, failure, forgiveness and some of the lessons I've learnt, all too slowly, from my experience thus far. And for the following hour I answered questions, and listened to the reflections of my audience. The evening was soon over. They applauded and I prayed for them before they were escorted back to their cells. But, as this was happening, one officer slipped forward and asked me if I would speak privately with one of the prisoners for a few minutes.

Nathan was in his early twenties. As we sat there, he thanked me for meeting him, and told me about how he would have loved to have met me five years earlier, before he got himself into trouble. He then explained quietly that he was a murderer. 'That's who I am,' he insisted. 'I am a murderer. End of story – full stop. I have wasted my life.'

I asked him to tell me more. When he was younger he had joined a gang. 'It wasn't safe to not belong. I joined up for protection.' He told me about the first time a gang member had turned up with a knife and how everyone else had been horrified. 'But the guy with the blade explained that the other gangs all carried knives and that the only way to be safe was to carry them too. We would never have to use them, but they would be a symbol of our strength which would send a message to everyone else – don't mess with us.'

Then he spoke of how one night, when he was seventeen, he was hanging around with his friends in the park, getting drunk, when a rival gang wandered in. Soon an alcohol-fuelled fight had broken out. He explained how one of the boys from the other gang pulled a knife out and came towards him. 'I recognised him. He used to be in my class at primary school. I realised he was going to stab me. I pulled my knife out and, before I knew it, somehow it was in him. I ran away. I was so scared. Later that night, I discovered he was dead before the ambulance even arrived.'

'So, I am a murderer. That's it,' he said. 'It's too late for me. But if I could, I'd tell all those kids, just like I was, to choose a different pathway; to learn from my story and my mistakes.' Nathan's time with me was up. Two guards arrived ready to escort him back to his cell. He turned to leave the hall.

He was almost out of the door when suddenly I realised what I needed to do. I shouted across the room. 'Wait. Wait. You've passed the interview.' Confused and slightly taken aback by my apparently random outburst, Nathan and his guards stopped in their tracks and gazed back at me. 'You've passed the interview,' I repeated. 'What interview?' he asked quizzically. 'The interview,' I replied.

From the puzzled expression on his face I could see I needed to clarify. 'The job interview you just had – you passed it!

Here's my name and email address, for when you get out of here. There's a job waiting for you as a community youth worker with Oasis. Congratulations; if you want it, you're a future Oasis staff member.'

We stood in silence for a moment. I watched as Nathan's body language slowly changed. His story had been subverted. His full stop had become nothing more than a comma. There was another clause to the sentence; another paragraph to the chapter; another chapter to the book – and it was called hope. Nathan had a goal, a purpose, a vision, a *telos* to his story!

Far too often, people get stuck in their stories: 'I'm illiterate.' 'I'm ugly.' 'I'm spoilt goods.' 'I have HIV and a death sentence hanging over me.' 'I'm trapped in addiction.' 'I'm unpopular.' 'I'm a mistake.' 'I'll never get to university – no one from my family has ever been before.' 'I didn't go to college, I'm not qualified for anything.' 'I'm thick.' 'I'm useless.' 'I've wasted my life.' 'I'm not wanted.' 'I'm too slow.' 'I'm too young.' 'I'm too old.' 'I'm no use to anyone.' 'I'm unemployable.' The problem with each of these statements is that they all end with a full stop. They are going nowhere. Each one is in search of a new *telos*: a new direction; a new goal. I have a friend who puts it this way: 'You can't start the next chapter of your life until you stop re-reading your last one.'

In reality, of course, we all live with conflicting stories about ourselves. A kind of internal civil war. These differing voices compete for our loyalty. Harmful stories, which seek to crush us, to remind us that we are nothing. Proud stories whose goal is to persuade us that life is about the labels we own and the wealth we accumulate, as they attempt to offer us the comfort that we are better than others. Arrogant stories that whisper to us of our prowess and indispensability. We have to choose, and keep choosing, which of these and other competing stories we believe and which we will live within.

There is a famous old saying in the Hebrew scriptures: 'Where there is no vision, the people perish'.[1] Without direction, we stagnate or get lost. If you start a journey facing in the wrong direction or without a map, it may not show up immediately, but eventually it will land you many miles from where you hoped to be. When we don't know where we're headed we meander at best.

To say it again – the greatest barrier to achievement is the inability to see. Our lack of imagination boxes us in. Or, to quote Albert Einstein again, 'If you can't imagine it, you can't do it.'[2]

The plot of every great novel was first sketched in the mind of its author before being committed to paper.

The lyrics of every wonderful song were first scribbled and then revised on a note pad before being performed in a concert hall.

The design of every magnificent building was first drawn on a piece of paper before it was built with stone, glass and steel.

In 1464, the sculptor Agostino di Duccio began work on a huge piece of marble quarried from the Italian Alps. But, because of a fault that ran right through it, he abandoned the project.

Ten years later, another sculptor, Antonio Rossellino, took up where Duccio had left off. But, within months, the problems posed by the massive block of marble, nicknamed 'The Giant', meant it was, once more, discarded – this time for another twenty-five years.

Later, the great Leonardo da Vinci was asked to consider tackling it, but, in the end, it was not until 16 August 1501 that Michelangelo, as a young twenty-six-year-old, received the commission to transform it; a daunting task that would absorb him for the next two years.

Today, *David*, portraying the famous biblical king at the moment he decided to do battle with Goliath, is without doubt the world's most iconic sculpture.

What was it that gave Michelangelo the ability to see what others were blind to? He put it this way: 'Every block of stone has a statue inside it and it's the task of the sculptor to discover it.'

If you can't imagine it, you can't do it.

I have a friend whose life fell apart. A series of rash, short-sighted decisions he made robbed him of his wife and children and left him abandoned, alone, jobless and homeless. Seeking work he moved to the city of Liverpool, but life just got harder. Eventually, in desperation, in the middle of a cold biting winter, and not knowing what else to do, he sought out the then Anglican Bishop of Liverpool, David Sheppard, at his palace. He knocked on the door, was shown in, and asked to wait. Minutes later the bishop appeared, made him a cup of tea and asked how he could help. My friend poured out his sorry tale – one filled with hopelessness, guilt and despair.

Having listened for a while, the bishop announced that he had to go out for a meeting for an hour or so, but told my friend that he was free to stay in the warm. He asked him to sit and reflect on the copy of the famous oil painting by Rembrandt, *The Return of the Prodigal Son* – depicting the homecoming of the wayward son in Jesus' famous story – that was hanging in his study. But as my friend sat gazing at it, searching for some hope within it, in the warmth he soon fell asleep. However, on waking up, his eyes fell on a feature within the painting he had never noticed before.

In the very centre of the Dutch master's painting are the hands of the father wrapped around his wayward and regretful son. In fact, Rembrandt concentrates all the light in his picture on them. But he has painted the two hands quite differently. The father's left hand is strong and muscular. Its fingers are spread out. It holds the son firmly.

The father's right hand is different. It does not hold or grasp. It is gentle. It strokes. It is refined and soft. It tenderly caresses the son's shoulder. It's a mother's hand. In the father's two hands, one masculine, the other feminine, mercy becomes reality; forgiveness, reconciliation and healing become tangible. Through them, not only the tired son but the worn-out father both find their rest.

For all the times that my friend had glanced at Rembrandt's work in the past, he had never seen this. He says that it was as though the scales fell from his eyes. His ailing imagination was rekindled. For the first time in years God's healing, tender and forgiving presence seemed tangible to him. He relaxed. He was at peace. He felt forgiven by a loving God; he even felt that he was able to forgive himself. No longer did he feel trapped by his past. He could see a new chapter and sensed new hope. He broke down in tears; tears of regret, relief, of homecoming and hope.

The disappointments and failures of life – a broken relationship, an illness, redundancy, failed ambition, rejection – often cause us to batten down the hatches against further pain or rejection. Our sense of awe and wonder shrinks. We become closed, cautious and suspicious. We contract. Stagnate. We are immobilised. We turn our backs on the adventure of life. We stop trusting. We stop growing. Pain and bitterness slowly form a cocoon in which we become encased. Only this makes us feel safe. We inhabit it and feed on it for the rest of our lives. It becomes our story – our way of seeing things.

Our culture is allergic to regret and guilt. 'You mustn't feel guilty. Guilt is repressive. Banish that negative thought. It's not your fault.' But, as Francis Spufford explains:

> If you won't hear the bad news about yourself, you can't know yourself. You condemn yourself to the maintenance of an exhausting illusion, a false front about yourself which keeps out doubt and with it hope, change, nourishment, breath, life. If you won't hear the bad news, you can't begin to hear the good news about yourself either.[3]

Our past is our past. It's out of reach. It's set in stone. The child you neglected grew up into the adult who will always be shaped, in part, by that neglect. The effort you failed to put into your first marriage has left you, and your ex-partner, with scar tissue that is now part of you both. The close friendship that you allowed to wither through your lack of investment of time or the inability to say sorry has died. None of this can be revisited, revised, relived or replaced.

But to acknowledge our failure, to look our guilt fairly and squarely in the eye rather than to ignore or deny it, can be the first step towards new hope; the beginning of our longed-for healing. The fundamental message of Jesus is that we are loved by God and, even in our most monumental failures, all that is required is that we wake up, turn around and journey home to his cleansing, forgiving, restoring love. God does not do guilt. God does forgiveness.

Dave Tomlinson tells the story of his conversation with a grieving woman about her mother, whose funeral he was preparing to take. He asked her if there was a story or incident that illustrated or encapsulated what her mother was like. After a brief pause, she replied:

> When I was a small child I broke a treasured vase, a family heirloom. Knowing how important it was, I screamed as it crashed to the floor and broke into a hundred pieces. But when my mother rushed into the room, she appeared relieved, not angry. Gathering me into her arms, she said, 'Thank God, I thought you were hurt.'

With tears in her eyes, the woman explained to Dave that this was what her mother was like, before she added, 'And that was the day I discovered that I was the family treasure.'[4]

This is the heart of the message of Jesus: we are God's family treasure. God loves us more than we can imagine. The stories of our brokenness are redeemed by seeing and accepting this different story about ourselves. My life was changed when I recognised that I was defined, not by my past actions, but by his love for me and my future potential as I allowed my small story to be caught up into his big story.

Like Albert Einstein said: 'Imagination is more important than knowledge.'

7

The Story that Shapes Us

Once you understand your story and its *telos*, it naturally begins to shape your responses, behaviour and habits. You begin to think about or 'anticipate' your ultimate goal in terms of your present behaviour.

Even though your favourite film is on TV at midnight, if you know that you have an interview for a job that is important to you in the morning, you anticipate it by turning off the television, thinking through your application again, sorting out the clothes you are planning to wear, and then getting an early night.

However, although expectation should create anticipation – it doesn't always do the job.

Someone's sense of expectation might tell them that, if they continue to be late for work, they run the risk of losing their job, but still make little impact on their arrival time.

Someone might have an expectation that by doing more physical exercise their health will improve, but still not quite make it away from the comfort of the couch and into the gym.

It's easy – far too easy – to get ourselves stuck; lulled into a place where our expectations fail to translate into real anticipation in terms of behaviour and habits.

It's only when the worker who is persistently late has 'seen' the written warning about their timekeeping that their expectation grows into a real belief that something has to change and they go to the local store and buy an extra-loud alarm clock!

It's only when the overweight 'couch-potato' 'sees' with their own eyes the medical report explaining, in black and white, that they are at risk of a heart attack that what has been a nagging unhappiness with their lifestyle turns into a firm commitment to changing their diet and signing up for a fitness class!

Once you really believe that something is going to happen – once you 'see' it – you begin to behave in a way that anticipates it.

A skilled driver will anticipate what is going to happen on the road in front of them and adjust their speed accordingly to compensate. A good tennis player will anticipate their opponent's shot by beginning to move into the right position before the ball has actually been struck. If I know that an important person will be visiting my office in the morning, I anticipate their arrival by tidying it up the night before.

There is no hiding it. What we believe, eventually and inevitably, becomes apparent through our attitudes, actions and habits. When we really *believe* something to be true it starts to impact on the way that we live; we begin to anticipate or to reflect it in the way we *behave*, the way we think and the way we use our time and resources. As the old saying explains, 'The apple never falls far from the tree.'

In a small corner of the ancient city of Prague, in central Europe, there is an old synagogue that now serves as a memorial to the 77,297 Jewish Czechoslovakian victims of Hitler's regime. At the outbreak of the Second World War in 1939, Prague was home to one of the largest Jewish communities in Europe. On 15 March, Germany occupied Czech lands. Some of the Czech Jewish community escaped and emigrated to various countries and regions, but not all were so fortunate.

Soon after the occupation of the country by the Germans, a set of humiliating anti-Jewish laws and policies began to be introduced. First the Jews were deprived of various civic freedoms, then their businesses and properties began to be taken, following this their freedom of movement around the city was withdrawn, and – in the end – the overwhelming majority of them found themselves deported to the Nazi extermination camps between 1941 and 1945.

The Pinkas Synagogue is one of the most evocative and heart-breakingly direct reminders of this tragedy. In a labour of love, the names of all those, from the surrounding region, who had their lives so cruelly taken away from them are inscribed on the building's interior walls. Each inscription is painstakingly and beautifully handwritten. And that so many of the entries contain names of young children – easily recognised because the dates of birth and death are also recorded – adds considerably to the poignancy and sense of tragedy.[1]

But, beyond the tragedy, these entries pose an even bigger question. Why are there so many names of children, toddlers and even babies on the list? Why, when Hitler is planning to destroy your people, when you already live imprisoned in a ghetto, when you have heard the rumours about the mass slaughter of your people in Nazi death camps, do you still have children?

There is only one answer to this question – one which to non-Jewish people may, at first, sound very strange: Torah.

The Torah, the ancient, holy text of the Jewish people, not only explains to them who they are, but it places their small individual stories in the context of the bigger overarching, meaning-giving story of their people and their destiny. And it's this framing story which has been retold week after week, year after year, century after century, by faithful Jews around the world. Indeed, in the story, God himself instructs the hearers to pass it on to their children.

> Fix these words of mine in your hearts and minds; tie them as symbols on your hands and bind them on your foreheads. Teach them to your children, talking about them when you sit at home and when you walk along the road, when you lie down and when you get up.[2]

And this is what the story they passed from generation to generation tells them about themselves:

> *I will make you into a great nation,*
> *and I will bless you;*
> *I will make your name great,*
> *and you will be a blessing.*
> *I will bless those who bless you,*
> *and whoever curses you I will curse;*
> *and all peoples on earth*
> *will be blessed through you.*[3]

When you believe a story like that, you know that Auschwitz can't be the end. When you believe a story like that, you know that even the Third Reich's 'Final Solution' – code for their planned extermination of the Jewish peoples – will never achieve its goal. When you believe a story like that, you know your people have a different destiny. When you believe a story like that, you know that you are a small part of a much bigger unfolding purpose.

The story we own, that we have come to believe about ourselves, may restrict and disempower us, robbing us of direction, but it may set us free and even in the darkest of situations bring us hope and help us to see the way ahead.

Perhaps our problem is that for the vast majority of our time we avoid the most important question; the only question that can really provide us with the fuel we need to live well. In the end, the most important question in life is 'why?' And the only way to answer it is to give yourself enough time and space to discover the story that you are called to live by, and then to have the courage to be obedient to its voice.

Alfred Nobel was born on 21 October 1833 in Stockholm. His father was an engineer and inventor.

In 1864, when Alfred was twenty-nine, his younger brother Emil and four other people were killed in a nitro-glycerine explosion in his family's Swedish factory. Dramatically affected by this event, Nobel, who had studied chemical engineering, set out to develop a safer explosive. This he patented in 1867 under the name of 'dynamite'.

Dynamite established Alfred's fame and was soon being used to blast tunnels, cut canals and build railways and roads all over the world. Nobel went on to invent a number of other explosives as well as to build a multi-million dollar fortune for himself.

But, twenty years later, in 1888, another extraordinary event was to shape Alfred's legacy. He was astonished to wake up one morning to read his own obituary. Following the death of another of his brothers, Ludvig, while visiting France, a leading newspaper there mistakenly published an obituary for Alfred, which it titled 'The merchant of death is dead'. It went on to condemn Alfred for his invention of dynamite, which was by then being used in military campaigns by armies around the world.

So horrified was Alfred by this depiction of his life's work, and how he now saw he would be remembered, that he was shocked into doing what he had always been too busy to do. He stopped to reflect on what his life was about – what was his story and how could he be obedient to it? As a result he set about changing his will, which when published after his own death eight years later of a stroke, in 1896, scandalised his relatives but changed the world's view of his life.

Alfred had left the bulk of his vast fortune – almost 95 per cent of it, worth around 250 million dollars – for the creation of the Nobel Foundation in order to establish a set of annual awards for 'those who, during the preceding year, shall have conferred the greatest benefit on mankind'. The prizes were to be for physics, chemistry, medicine, literature and, of course, most famous of all – for working towards peace![4]

Unlike Alfred Nobel, we are not very likely to have the opportunity to read our own obituaries. But, just like him, each of us authors the story we will be remembered for. Day by day, year by year, we write our legacy line by line. And as the story we choose to live by and its *telos* becomes part of us, we become part of it and our lives are governed and shaped by it.

8

A New Agenda

So, the big question is this: how do we imagine and then write the story we want to live in?

How do we live 'on purpose'?

How do we become the person that we want to be?

There is a short-sightedness – or perhaps an incompleteness – in the advice given to so many of us in our early years. I'm saddened when I meet a young person who seems to have little aspiration for their life – no grasp of their enormous potential. But I'm equally troubled by the partial nature or lopsidedness of so much of the 'professional' advice that's constantly on offer. 'Raise your sights', 'study hard', 'you could become an architect, a lawyer, an accountant, a doctor, a teacher or the prime minister'. It is as though we've fallen into the trap of believing that 'status' brings with it an automatic pass to fulfilment and well-being.

How many highly paid professionals reach middle age, washed up and with no sense of direction or motivation? For them life now feels like a perpetual gym session on a treadmill where you can run as hard as you like but still go nowhere.

How many successful, married men or women 'get involved' with 'someone else' and end up divorced or separated, only to recognise, on reflection, that their affair was not because they were bored with their partner but, at root, because they were bored with themselves?

How many people wake up one morning, look around and say: 'How did I get here? This isn't who I was going to be!'?

'Life consists of two journeys,' says my friend Dave Tomlinson,

> the outward journey of the body through time and space, and an inner journey of the soul. The outward journey creates the shell of our existence: where we live, what sort of work we do, whether or not we have a partner or children, what sort of things we spend our time on, all of which are very important aspects of our life. But the inner journey focuses on creating depth to our existence: discovering who we really are, establishing a sense of meaning and purpose to life, finding our moral and spiritual compass, deciding what it is that drives us.[1]

The questions 'Who am I?' and 'What is living for?' are the most important a person can ask argues Professor Anthony Kronman, the former Dean of Yale University.[2] Education has to be more than a preparation for a career. It must also explore the art of living – the spiritual question of how we ought to live our lives. But, he claims, this issue about what makes life worth living has been largely abandoned in our mad rush to gain 'qualifications'.

Writing from the context of American university education Kronman contrasts our own times with an earlier era, when the question of the meaning of life was right at the very centre of the curriculum. He suggests that teachers, who in generations past once felt a special responsibility to guide their students in exploring the question of what living is for, have lost confidence in their authority to do so. But more than that, he reflects, they have lost sight of the question itself in the blinding fog of political correctness that now dominates their disciplines.

Today, students can find courses devoted to every subject under the sun. There is only one question for which most of them will search their curriculum catalogues in vain: the question of the meaning of life; of what you should care about and why; of what living is for.

> In a shift of historic importance, America's colleges and universities have largely abandoned the idea that life's most important question is an appropriate subject for the classroom. In doing so, they have betrayed their students by depriving them of the chance to explore it in an organized way, before they are caught up in their careers and preoccupied with the urgent business of living itself.[3]

He believes that what we desperately need now is what we once had: an approach to education that takes these matters seriously without pretending to have instant, 'pre-packaged' answers to them all.

Kronman, who is not religious, suggests that the best way to explore the answers to these vital questions is to study the great works of philosophy, literature and art, in which they are presented with lasting beauty and strength. 'The fundamentalists have the wrong answer', he writes, 'but they've got the right questions. We need to learn to ask them again.'

He argues that we neglect these social, emotional, spiritual and moral questions, not only to our individual cost, but also to that of our communities and of society itself. 'When we ignore life's biggest questions', he says, 'we all pay the price.'

Perhaps no episode in modern history speaks louder of this than the tragedy of the Jewish Holocaust under Hitler's Third Reich. How could the most sophisticated nation in the most advanced century in history stoop to such barbarism? How could Nazi Germany become, at one and the same time, scientifically brilliant and morally bankrupt? How could a system which could spawn first-class students in civil engineering and medicine, fail to nurture the kind of graduates with the backbone to refuse to use their knowledge to design the laboratories, gas chambers and ovens of Dachau and Auschwitz?

'It was methodical and systematic and conducted with cold efficiency by men [and women] who read poetry and listened to string quartets afterwards', writes Paul Vallely.

> Architects planned the camps – an interesting challenge, presumably, for no one had designed this kind of concentration camp before. Sewage engineers surveyed them, installing drainage ditches in the marshland and effluent treatment plants to avoid polluting local rivers. Rail officials timetabled the steady influx of trains to Birkenau, selected by Himmler for its good railway links.
>
> This was extermination on an industrial scale and it involved huge numbers of people. Neighbours and employers reported Jews to the Gestapo. Bureaucrats processed notices of deportation. Postmen served them. Railway staff marshalled their departure. Others drove the trains and manned the signals. It was all logically and legally planned in an inversion of all the values on which human civilisation had been built.[4]

Michael Polanyi, a brilliant Hungarian Jewish chemist, lived and worked in Berlin at the Kaiser Wilhelm Institute of Science during the years leading up to the Second World War, but eventually chose to flee Germany for England, only narrowly escaping the ghettos and concentration camps where millions of his fellow Jews would be annihilated over the coming years.

In his book *Personal Knowledge*, published in 1958, after much reflection on all this Polanyi argues that Germany's moral bankruptcy was at least partly due to the ideals of the Enlightenment, which had led to the popular belief that all knowledge could be discovered by individuals, through scientific research and reason alone.

The Enlightenment is the term that is often used to describe a phase in Western philosophy and cultural life which centred on developments in eighteenth-century Europe, when many thinkers began to emphasise the importance of science and reason as the primary source of authority. Empirical knowledge – the objective, measurable, verifiable, evidence-based, data-driven world of cold scientific facts, processes and cast-iron certainty – slowly became all that mattered; the basis of all thought and progress.[5]

Germany, and especially Berlin, stood in the vanguard of this movement, and with it, German university life began to be centred around the novel assumption, without precedent in the history of education, that it existed primarily to sponsor this empirical research and that its chief responsibility was simply to provide the space, books, expertise and other resources needed to produce this new knowledge.

At one level, the adoption of this innovative way of learning achieved astounding results – particularly in terms of the sciences.[6] One of its by-products, however, was that interest in the world of the spiritual and untouchable, and the question of life's meaning, declined and was eventually excluded from serious academic concern all together as being too subjective, too unformed, too unmeasurable, too personal, to be the subject of specialised research.

In a world which banishes life's most important question we are all left impoverished. We are all de-humanised.

More latterly however, in our 'post-modern' society, we have begun to remind ourselves that life is about far more than equations and facts; a human being is more than a brain which simply thinks. We engage with life through the entirety of who we are. We play, we dance, we paint, we sing, we write, we watch, we touch, we serve, we build, we listen, we taste, we observe. As Albert Einstein famously put it, we have discovered that: 'Not everything that can be counted counts, and not everything that counts can be counted.'

Abraham Maslow, the American psychologist, is best known for his theory of self-actualisation, which describes the stages of

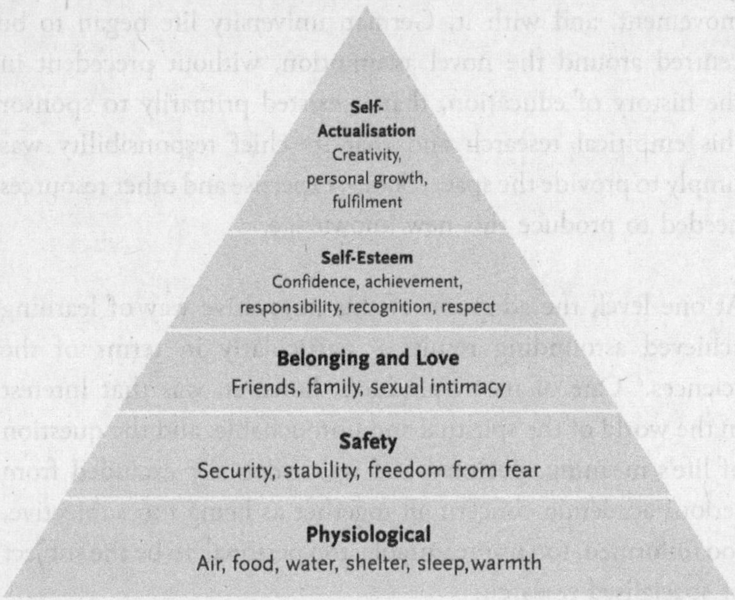

personal growth through which all humans pass. Popularly known as 'Maslow's Hierarchy of Needs' it suggests that human needs are arranged hierarchically on five levels. Maslow listed these in the form of what is now his famous pyramid to explain that our basic desires (the bottom ones), such as food, water and sleep, must be met before the higher categories begin to be considered.[7]

For Maslow, self-actualisation was about becoming 'fully human'.[8] It was about realising your potential; becoming everything that you are capable of becoming.

In the last years of his life, however, Maslow proposed the existence of a sixth level of needs that sat above and beyond those of self-actualisation. He named this category 'self-transcendence', which he said was concerned with the realm of spirituality. Indeed, he went as far as to assert that, in his view, it was only this final level that separated us from animals.

The pursuit of spirituality, as Maslow saw it, was humanity's crowning glory – sitting above and beyond his five lower categories. But, in reality, this quest for self-transcendence also defies the neat hierarchical nature of his basic thesis. Many of the clearest and strongest expressions of dynamic spirituality through history have arisen from those living in the depths of pain, poverty, oppression and injustice – those for whom the 'lower' needs of life have not been met.

In every human heart there is a deep longing for spirituality, which is frequently focused by need rather than comfort, and pain rather than contentment.

Around the beginning of the last century, psychologists began to experiment with ways of trying to measure intelligence. And, of course, following the ideas of the Enlightenment, IQ (Intelligence Quotient) – our capacity to process and apply knowledge in a rational fashion – became the definitive method of assessing this. Indeed, for most of the century IQ was regarded as the only sort of intelligence that mattered!

But how many times have you met someone who is hugely intellectual and loaded with letters after their name but socially awkward and an emotional 'cold fish'?

Responding to all this, and to the sobering lessons that were slowly beginning to sink in from the world wars of the first half of the twentieth century, in 1983 Howard Gardner first put forward the theory of multiple intelligences.[9] Though someone may not have any great mathematical skill, they might, for example, have strong musical or outstanding artistic intelligence.

In the mid-1990s, another scholar, Daniel Goleman, popularised research that showed that Emotional Intelligence (EQ) is of equal importance to IQ. EQ, he said, enables empathy and compassion and creates the ability for a person to respond to the needs of others. It allows those who are strong in it to read other people and their situations and feelings, but also creates an increased level of self-awareness.

Then, in 1997, Danah Zohar[10] coined another new term, Spiritual Intelligence – and with it introduced the idea of a third 'Q'! SQ drives us to explore the big questions: Why am I here? What is the purpose of life? Which path should I follow? 'SQ is concerned with the inner life of mind and spirit and its relationship to being in the world.'[11] It allows us to dream and to strive. We use it to develop our longing and capacity for meaning, vision and value. And to ignore, or to avoid, this inner journey leaves us with a nagging sense of emptiness as we struggle with an absence of meaning in our lives.[12]

According to Stephen Covey, the famous educator and businessman, 'Spiritual intelligence is the central and most fundamental of all the intelligences, because it becomes the source of guidance for the others.'[13] But it might come as a shock to some to discover that it's quite possible to be extremely pious and religious, and yet have a very low level of SQ. On the other hand, there are countless people who, though they would not regard themselves as at all religious, are rich in spiritual intelligence. For them, the quest for prosperity and status has been superseded by the search for purpose and fulfilment as they have learnt to reflect more deeply on the purpose of life.

There's a joke that says, 'A religious fundamentalist is someone who is awfully worried that there is someone out there, somewhere, who is having fun.' And a tragedy is that the well-known term 'repent' has popularly become wrapped up with this same kind of long-faced, judgemental approach to life; synonymous with a summons to wipe the smile off your face, stop misbehaving and get some religion.

The challenge to repentance on the lips of Jesus, however, was never about any of this kind of 'there's nothing to smile about' approach to life. Instead, it was, and remains, simply a call to wake up and live life to the full! It is about adopting a new story. It is about living differently, living bigger, with wonder in your eyes; expanding your horizons – it's like beginning again. Like being born again – which, of course, is exactly what Jesus meant when he used that phrase, rather than all the religious nonsense that some have laid over it since.

The Greek word *metanoia*, from which our word 'repentance' is translated, literally means 'to think differently after' – it's about a second thought with hindsight, which is different from, as well as wiser and more grounded than, the former thought. It denotes a change of mind or change of heart based on a greater awareness and perception.[14] It's about SQ.

So, for instance, the Jewish historian Josephus, who was born a few years after Jesus' crucifixion, recounts how, as a young Roman army officer, he was sent to Galilee in AD 66 to sort out a bunch of Judean revolutionaries – intent on the violent overthrow of their Roman oppressors – who were beginning to annoy the Empire. In his autobiography, he explains how he rode into Galilee to attempt a face-to-face meeting with this handful of terrorists who, with inadequate resources, were ready and willing, but totally unable, to take on the military might of the Imperial Roman machine. Josephus realised that their hot-headedness amounted to nothing less than a suicide mission. So, at the risk of his own life, he tried to persuade the rebels that there was an alternative – a wiser and better way of seeing and doing things.

Josephus describes how, on meeting the Jewish rebel leader, he pleaded with him to give up his short-sighted agenda, to wake up, to think differently and to trust him to find a better way forward. He and his men would never achieve the freedom they craved if they continued with their violent plan. The actual words Josephus used, however, were simply: 'Repent and believe in me.'[15]

Jesus often used the word 'repent'. 'The time has come. The kingdom of God has come near. Repent and believe the good news!' are his very first recorded words in Mark's Gospel (1:15). But it's not there to tell us off; to put us down and to rub it in. Rather, it's to encourage us to make better choices, in line with the vision we own – the story we choose to live within.

Jesus was saying, 'Wake up. Turn your thinking around. Start living your life differently. Do it my way! Your way won't work. Choose mine instead!' That's precisely what people heard: a call to a new agenda, a different way of doing life – a bigger and better vision for life than anyone else had previously articulated.

'Take it or leave it', 'Like it or lump it', 'It's just the way I am', 'I can't help it' and 'You can't teach an old dog new tricks' are all well-known phrases in our culture. But, as popular, even ubiquitous, as these sentiments are, they fly in the face of the truth. They are really all just elaborate ways of saying

'I can't be bothered', 'I'm not interested', 'I'm sticking with what I've got'.

Wake up!

Repent! Explore your SQ! Do life differently!

9

Life is Not an Exam

I was in my mid-twenties and working for a church in Kent, where part of my job was to visit some of its older members who were no longer capable of getting out and about or attending our Sunday worship services. Every Tuesday afternoon, like clockwork, I followed the same routine, visiting Mrs Ball and Mrs Blackburn, two very different, very elderly, widows who'd both been members of the church for over sixty years.

Part of my responsibility was to take these two ladies a recording of the previous Sunday morning's service as well as to pick up the one that I'd left with them the week before. My first visit was the hard one. Mrs Ball was in her mid-eighties and was always angry. Every week she'd launch into a withering critique of the service she'd listened to over the previous seven days. First, she'd object to the songs and music, then she'd let me know that she didn't like the prayers. She'd go on to disagree with the content of the sermon and the style in which it was delivered and use all this as an entry point into an elongated moan about the state of the church and society in general. I always left her feeling worn down and slightly deflated.

My second visit was to Norah Blackburn. It was like chalk and cheese. Norah was kind, generous, cheerful, interested in what was going on and asked questions about children, the youth group, the church leaders and the wider community. She'd always thank me for coming and usually comment on how much she'd enjoyed listening to last week's service. She wasn't afraid to let me know if she disagreed with the sermon – especially if it was one of mine – but she was always positive, affirming, thoughtful and gentle. I always left Norah feeling better about life, myself and the world in general.

I've never forgotten those two women. From them I learnt this. In the end, you become what you've practised being. Though at first we choose the story we live in, as the years go by the story we have chosen ends up shaping us.

It seems strange to say it, but if we think that ethics are only about debating big issues like religion, international justice, the environment, the economy, business, education, healthcare and poverty, or about dealing with moments of personal crisis, we make a huge mistake.

Ethics are about the whole process of becoming the sort of person you want to be. Ethics are essentially about everyday life – our passions and perceptions – and the slow cultivation of good habits and moral skills. All of which means that, in short, every moment, even the most mundane, is an opportunity for moral formation and spiritual development, as slowly but surely we grow into the people that our chosen way of life shapes the raw material that is us into.

Our character leaks out through our attitudes when we are not paying attention. It bubbles to the surface. We wear it on our faces. It shines from our eyes. It is audible in our tone. It can't be hidden – it catches us off guard. It is the real us, and it always seeps and trickles out of us, however hard we work. There is no hiding it.

The problem is that the way many people think about ethics neglects the only time we can use to make a real difference. In a crisis, it is only the habits that we have already formed, day by day, over the years, that can help us. In fact, many of the impossibly big moral dilemmas some of us find ourselves in wouldn't arise at all if we had a different ethical foundation in the first place.

It is a little like trying to carry a bucket of water filled to the brim up a steep hill without spilling any of its contents. It is impossible, however hard you concentrate. And if, halfway up, someone unexpectedly bumps into you and knocks you off balance, the result is disaster. It is inevitable. There's no containing it. What's inside slops out everywhere!

As we are regularly reminded, we are human 'beings' not human 'doings'. So, how do we build the key skills we need for life, not just the skills for a job; skills that will develop our character – our EQ and our SQ – rather than just our IQ?

Through the centuries humanity has wrestled with the question of the best way to deal with this issue. How do we live well? And though countless theories have been developed, in the end they all boil down to just three options.

Option one: Live by the rule book.[1]
Option two: The end justifies the means – so do what seems best.[2]
Option three: Live in a story.[3]

The various 'rule book' theories place their emphasis on obedience to a chosen set of moral absolutes.[4] The idea is that, using these as a measure, any behaviour can be instantly judged as inherently good or evil. So, for instance, if we regard truth-telling as an 'absolute', we have an unchanging duty to do exactly that, at all times, regardless of the outcome.[5]

In practice, of course, rigidly keeping any set of rules or regulations is an inflexible, wooden and unrealistic way to try to determine how to live. If always telling the truth is non-negotiable, not only is it sometimes incredibly insensitive (take, for instance, the famous dilemma when someone you care about asks you, 'How do I look in this? I bought it especially for tonight'), it can also become highly inappropriate, destructive and even immoral (as in the prying question: 'Tell me all you know about his/her past').

And then there's the problem of which rule should take priority when two of the rules that undergird your ethical system clash. For instance, if always telling the truth is essential to your worldview, but you also have a commitment to love others, what do you say to a would-be murderer who asks where his next intended victim is hiding and you know the answer?

If all that wasn't enough, there's another huge problem with a rule-book approach. You are forced to keep inventing new rules for unforeseen or nuanced situations. And the more you have, the more like a badly fitting, inflexible, unbending, suffocating and eventually deadly straitjacket it all becomes.[6] Whenever you lay down a rigid set of rules, you instantly exclude all kinds of creative possibilities.

A few years ago, one of my sons borrowed my bike – which was a very distinctive bright orange in colour – and had it stolen in London. He reported it to the police. It was processed and he was given what he was told was an all-important crime reference number. Some months later my other son, who was working for the police at the time, happened to be in a South London police station where he spotted my lost bike. It had been recovered in a drugs raid. He phoned me and told me to go and claim it.

Excitedly, the next day I attended the station, filled in a complex form, gave the staff our original crime reference number, walked outside into the yard and identified the bike – it was unmistakable. I even touched it! But it was locked up and, I was told, only the constable in charge of the case could fill in the relevant paperwork and release it to me, and he was away on holiday.

To cut a tediously long – and extraordinarily frustrating – story short, over the next eighteen months I phoned, visited and emailed the police station on numerous occasions, in a futile attempt to reclaim my bike. But nothing worked. Reluctantly, in the end, I realised that it was costing me so much time and energy to absolutely no avail that I cut my losses, gave up and bought a new bike!

I have no reason to believe that there was ever a plot to keep my bike – though some suggested it! The police I dealt with were far from corrupt. All the constables and the local sergeant I spoke to were perfectly polite and friendly. This was no conspiracy against me; instead, it was just a wooden commitment to obeying all the regulations of the system in which common sense, justice and a concern about the outcome were overwhelmed by 'jobsworth' rule keeping.

Another reason that an inflexible obedience to the rules doesn't work is because they all tell us about the world that used to be, rather than the one into which we are heading. Rules codify the past. They were designed to deal with what happened yesterday and try to extract or distil the lessons that were learnt from the experience. They are, of their very nature, a map of the past.

No map is ever more than a snapshot of a moment in time. A cartographer's life is a frustrating one; as fast as they update their work, it is out of date again. The landscape of all towns and cities is constantly under development, so it's a serious mistake to confuse any map for reality. Whenever you look at a map, you have to remember that it is not the thing itself – it is no more than an approximation to it. The same is true for the software that comes as part of their digital navigation equivalents in cars!

Though none of this renders maps useless, it does mean that, unless we are prepared to redraw or reprogram them on a regular basis, we are destined to peer through them at a world which bears a diminishing relationship to anything they purport to represent. And this, of course, can become very dangerous for both drivers and their passengers, when the road layout ahead has been re-modelled, but the map or navigation system they are using has not!

As Mark Twain put it, 'History doesn't repeat itself – at best it sometimes rhymes', which is why rules are helpful as guides to the way ahead but often fail to give you enough information and insight to make the wisest decisions.

The Ten Commandments are probably one of the most misread and misunderstood pieces of literature in the world, and a clear illustration of exactly this point. You can't read the Bible or any other text properly, without taking its setting, culture, context and developing narrative, or story, seriously. You can never get at the truth of a text without the hard work of dealing with the circumstances of the story in which it is set. You can't just yank verses or passages out of their historical context and apply them, without the great risk of misapplying them. But, by any account, these 'commands' were never an exhaustive list of rules and regulations capable of guiding Israel safely through every ethical decision they would ever face, as is evidenced by the fact that the Old Testament contains just over six hundred other laws in what is often known as the Mosaic code.

Though the commandments are often portrayed as a list of tough requirements that a demanding deity insists are kept before he will bless his people, this is to seriously misunderstand both them and the God who gave them. Rather than rigid rules they highlight a set of values designed to guide and govern the community's life together.

The commandments were never intended as a prerequisite to finding God's favour, a list of essential qualifications for 'being blessed'. Rather they are God saying, 'I love you unconditionally and I've already demonstrated that to you. You were slaves, brick-makers, no-hopers back in Egypt. But I've lifted you out of your slavery and given you freedom and a new beginning; a new hope. So trust me. Live like this. Follow me. Copy me. Reflect who I am to the whole world – the God of love and mercy. I got you out of Egypt; these principles are designed to get Egypt out of you.'[7]

So, with the Ten Commandments as a centrepiece, God then supplied Israel with an ethic for the whole of life.[8] Time and again this 'law' asserted his uniqueness as the God of love, and called on those who believed in him to act in accordance with that revelation.

Take, for instance, the well-known and frequently quoted saying, 'an eye for an eye, a tooth for a tooth', so often used, even today, to justify retaliation. Possibly no other Old Testament text has been the victim of more misunderstanding and exaggeration than this one. But when it is placed against the cultural backdrop of the brutal practices of the surrounding nations – including Egypt – at the time, it takes on a dramatic new meaning. It becomes a unique ethic of constraint put in place to limit, rather than justify, excessive violence and vengeful punishment, and bring a sense of justice.[9] In a world filled with a 'You take my son's tooth, I'll take your life and wipe out your whole family' approach to conflict resolution, it was revolutionary.

It is clear that Jesus understood the primary function of the commandments and wider law in exactly this way: to play their part in slowly helping to shape a moral vision, based on God's character, rather than to give us a list of rigid regulations to live by.

Like every boy in his culture, Jesus spent much of his youth learning the Jewish law. And he learnt it well. In fact, his knowledge of it amazed even the leading teachers of the day.[10] But as an adult, his own teaching, built on the strong foundation of having internalised it, went way beyond a rigid adherence to what he'd learnt as a child.

So, when asked for his view on the most important commandment by a legal expert[11] – and being perfectly aware that there were ten perfectly good ones to choose from – he did an extraordinary thing. He ignored them all and came up with something else: 'Love the Lord your God with all your heart and with all your soul and with all your mind.' Then, to really add insult to injury, having only been asked for just one, he went on, unprompted, to offer a second: 'Love your neighbour as yourself.'[12]

What he was really saying was, 'Love God. Love your neighbour the way you love yourself. That's it. That's what it means to be fully alive; a fully actualised human being. All the rest is window dressing. Every religious rule and precept is really just an attempt to contextualise what love looks like in practice in a given cultural setting.'[13]

The religious leaders of Jesus' day were terribly worried that if you gave up on the rules, you would be giving up on discipline. They didn't take well to the way in which he ignored their time-honoured interpretations of scripture. As far as they were concerned, his views, indeed his whole way of life, was blasphemous and heretical – which is why they wanted him silenced.

But Jesus knew that life is not primarily about rules – even for those who claim it is; it's about the development of habits and practices that are based on the story you've come to own. Rather than living by the endless rules – taking them at face value and mindlessly applying them without any thought of their original context or purpose – Jesus constantly seeks to demonstrate that what God really wants is for people to live within the spirit rather than the letter of the rules.

Jesus is trying to get people to recognise that the law is not enough. It might be a useful guide but it is never sufficient.

The rules may not always be relevant in every time and place, and, indeed, there may not be an actual rule we can point to for the specific situation we are facing. However, the principles behind the rules – mercy, justice, faithfulness, generosity, compassion, fortitude, patience, integrity (which are all outworkings of love) – are constantly applicable to life because they flow directly from the story of the giver of life: the God of love.

This love that Jesus is referring to is not, of course, about feelings and warm emotions. It isn't even necessarily dependent on liking the other person. This is why Jesus also taught us to love our enemies. The principle of loving your neighbour wasn't some later – slightly more considered and reduced – version of his more ambitious challenge to love our enemies. Instead, it was simply that Jesus' definition of neighbour is so wide that it embraces enemies.[14] Love is a choice, an act of the will, a decision to work for the well-being of the other, even when it means sacrificing our own well-being.

Every parent understands exactly the principle that Jesus was highlighting. Our children begin life with a series of hard, fast and necessary rules: never speak to strangers, don't cross the road on your own, never play with matches, no staying up past bedtime – and rightly so.[15] But, of course, all adults need to be able to speak to strangers, cross the road without a companion, use matches and learn how to balance getting a regular eight hours' sleep against work deadlines and social invitations.

The Dalai Lama once summed it up this way: 'We must learn the law very well, in order to know how to break it properly.'

And there's one final reason that there has to be a better way of living than just blind obedience to a set of rules.

Life is not an exam!

10

Throw Out the Rule Book

So if living by the rule book doesn't work, what about option two?

'It's about time that we let people be true to themselves and their own values,' a well-respected member of the British House of Lords declared on national radio recently. 'Be yourself. We've lived with repression for too long. Responsible, educated people should be free to do what comes naturally to them. We should give them the space to be authentic,' she argued, implying along the way, of course, that 'not doing what comes naturally' and 'not being true to yourself' is somehow very damaging and destructive.

'The end justifies the means, so just be authentic' approach to life and ethics developed as a response to all the repressive and ineffective rule-keeping approaches of the past. Consequentialism, to give it its proper name, comes in various shades. Rather than choosing to measure the morality of an action by whether the rules are kept, instead it is assessed by asking whether its goal is to achieve the greatest good possible for the greatest number of people possible. However, as worthy as this might at first sound, it doesn't take long to realise that, in practice, this 'just trust yourself and hope for the best' approach to living has at least as many serious pitfalls as the rule-book method that it was born in reaction to.[1]

As I listened to the radio, I reflected on the irony of the fact that the person speaking – a member of the House of Lords, the second house of the British parliament – has a role that is all about making rules and enforcing them. More than that, this particular lady happens to use her position to champion the rights and opportunities of elderly people very effectively.

I realised that what the baroness actually meant was: Let people be true to themselves and their own values as long as that involves safeguarding a society that honours the elderly. For instance, not cutting or restricting the National Health Service, guaranteeing that pensions are index linked, creating legislation that keeps the needs of those who are old central, never entertaining any concessions to the euthanasia lobby, and carefully monitoring all policy to ensure that 'progress' never creates age discrimination or tramples on the well-being of the most vulnerable in our society in any other way.

Part of the problem about being free to express yourself as you choose is that virtues aren't the only things that are habit-forming. The more someone behaves in a way that is damaging to themselves or to others, the more natural it will both seem to be and actually become. In the words of Tom Wright, 'Spontaneity, left to itself, can begin by excusing bad behaviour and end by congratulating vice.'[2]

We've all seen what happens when we allow people to just be themselves with the hope that it will work out well. What happens when the self to which someone wants to be true is the self that wants to cheat everyone they meet out of as much money as possible? What happens when the self I want to be true to is violent, abusive and dishonest? How do we respond to the drug-dealer, people trafficker, pickpocket, serial adulterer, paedophile, rapist or tax-evader who wants the freedom to be themselves?

However popular, in Western culture, the push towards 'freedom' and 'authenticity' may be, it simply does not make sense in terms of providing a serious moral framework in which to find fulfilment as individuals, let alone as communities or society as a whole.

I am, of course, very aware that to express this kind of view often earns those who dare to voice it the label 'killjoy'. But anyone who, because of family or friends, has had to cope with the deep and long-lasting bruises, wounds and scars left by some of the 'freedoms' to 'be and do what I want to do, when I want to do it' knows differently.

Community or church leaders, like me, are often thought of as 'killjoys' for voicing concern about the dangers of, for instance, promiscuity or greed. In my experience, however, the real killing of joy comes with the short-sighted and often self-centred grabbing of these pleasures. It's a bit like running up a big bill on a credit card. It might, as the advert used to say, 'take the waiting out of wanting', but the debt incurred has huge, ongoing and unwelcome repercussions until it is eventually paid off.[3]

To change the metaphor, on the one hand our lives are blighted by trying to phone in to a call line about a problem we're having with a product we purchased that doesn't work and the frustration of talking to someone at the other end of the phone who has been trained to 'follow the rule book' by asking a certain series of questions, without any deviation, however irrelevant they are.

On the other, though we say that we crave freedom to 'do our own thing', we recognise that in order for a state to retain political freedom, it is essential that there are forces of law and order to hold back theft and violence, to defend life and property, and to prevent the powerful or the malicious from oppressing the weak and vulnerable. Without these restraints, 'freedom' becomes an excuse for the licence of some and the repression of others.

Martin Luther King summed it up when he said: 'It may be true that the law cannot make a man love me, but it can stop him from lynching me, and I think that's pretty important.' The acceptance of appropriate moral constraints is not about curtailing true freedom, but rather about creating the environment in which it can flourish for all. To opt for one over the other is to throw the baby out with the bathwater – but the problem is to know when to apply which.

We need something deeper to guide us – something more captivating and persuasive than the dead hand of the rule book; something more trustworthy and reliable than our transient thoughts and feelings.

The phone-hacking scandal, dubbed 'hack-gate' by the press, began in 2005 with allegations that employees of the tabloid newspaper *News of the World* had illegally intercepted voicemail messages from the phones of celebrities, politicians and members of the British Royal Family. However, in July 2011, it was revealed that, more than this, the phones of murdered schoolgirl Milly Dowler, relatives of deceased British soldiers, and victims of the 7/7 London bombings had also been accessed. This resulted in a public outcry against News Corporation (the publisher of the newspaper) and its owner Rupert Murdoch, which, that same month, led to its closure, ending 168 years of publication.[4]

Eventually, even Murdoch's own daughter Elisabeth went public with her verdict on the family business: 'Profit without purpose is a recipe for disaster. Profit must be our servant not our master.' She concluded that what was sorely needed by the newspaper industry was 'a rigorous set of values based on an explicit statement of purpose'.[5]

Take, as another example, the ongoing string of scandals that have rocked the banking world over recent years. Deregulation has simply not worked and the call is for a new code of regulation to get us back on track. But, as Paul Tucker, a deputy governor of the Bank of England, speaking to an audience gathered beneath the dome of St Paul's Cathedral said, the problem is that introducing new and relevant rules – although very important – doesn't ever get to the heart of the problem. 'If it is correct that we won't write a perfect set of rules – we didn't in the past and we won't in the future – then there needs to be some other constraint, something that deals with values in a more basic sense.'[6]

At the same event, Stephen Green, chairman of HSBC and of the British Bankers' Association, agreed:

> The [banking] industry collectively owes the real world an apology for what has happened and it also owes the real world a commitment to learn the lesson . . . [but] this is not just about rules and regulations. You have to expect the leadership of the industry to nurture a real culture of ethics and integrity and that's the greatest priority of all for the boards of banks.

That's the problem. Neither regulation nor deregulation – the rules or the consequences approach to making ethical decisions – works. Not only are they too simplistic to cope with the complexity of life, but, at root, they both fail to deal with the real issue at the heart of every moral choice: the character of the people involved in making it. Doing your own thing – based on your own instincts – isn't good enough, but on the other hand, relying on a set of pre-ordained rules, by themselves, doesn't solve the problem either. What we need is not better rules – but better people.

It is only character development – the transforming and shaping of a life and its habits – that has the power to generate the sort of behaviour that both the rule book and the consequences approach might point towards but can never achieve. This is what the only other option – the 'live the story' approach to life – is all about.

Only *this* approach asks us the key question; the most important question in life. What type of person do you want to develop into? What kind of person are you becoming? Only *it* understands that our actions and responses are, to a great extent, an 'external' reflection of our 'internal' selves. Only *it* grasps that ethics is a way of seeing and understanding ourselves and our role in the world before it is a matter of doing anything.

An old man, whose journey through life had taught him much about becoming the person he was meant to be, was wandering through the forest one day, when he stumbled on a precious stone. He picked it up and put it into his bag.

Later he met a traveller and, in conversation with him, showed it to him. When the traveller saw the jewel, he demanded that it be handed over to him. The old man smiled and did so readily.

The traveller rushed off, overjoyed – the precious stone was enough to give him wealth for the rest of his life. However, a few days later he returned, found the old man and gave him back the stone.

'I want you to give me something far more precious than this stone . . . Give me whatever it was that enabled you to give me the stone in the first place.'

11
In Pursuit of Excellence

'You either have it or you don't.' It's an old myth, but it's persistent. It refuses to go away. But character formation – the shaping of a life and its habits – just like the development of any other talent, is a process, not a 'given'. And it is never too late to start!

All too often 'talent' gets defined simply as a 'natural ability', and with that huge assumption comes a gigantic misconception that continues to build itself right into the heart of our culture. From 'gifted' footballers, swimmers, sprinters, poets, writers, golfers and painters to 'genius' chess-players, magicians, dancers, artists, golfers, gymnasts, violinists, computer programmers and negotiators – we put success down to being born with excellence encoded in our DNA. And we make just the same mistake about good character.

We convince ourselves that talent and kindness, skills and spiritually, or the lack of them, are pre-ordained in just the same way as eye colour or shoe size. Our sporting, academic, artistic, vocational and social competence and achievement, or otherwise, are, with a little bit of luck thrown in, basically down to our genetic inheritance. There is absolutely nothing we can do about it all – it's just the way we are.

Take, for instance, the world of sport and David Beckham's legendary ability to bend the ball into the net or Michael Jordan's to fly through the air, magnetically draw towards the hoop. They, we believe, were born with something the rest of us missed out on – they were gifted. It all came to them naturally.

But recent research tells us that's not quite the way it is.

We are beginning to understand that the real difference between those who excel – in any discipline – and those who don't has much more to do with persistence and practice, determination and encouragement, than we had previously thought. From Scrabble enthusiasts to soccer players, and violinists to veterinary surgeons, all the research shows that 'those who achieve the most not only spend enormous, life-altering amounts of time and daily commitment to becoming better, but also exhibit a consistent – and persistent – style of preparation'.[1]

Kids become great footballers because they have a vision of being like their heroes. And it's that story that drives them to spend hour after hour kicking a ball up against a wall or learning to juggle it with their feet.

According to three-time Commonwealth table tennis champion, Matthew Syed:

> If we were to examine the incalculable hours of practice; the thousands of baby steps taken by world-class performers to get to the top, the skills would not seem quite so mystical or so inborn. Indeed, extensive research has shown that there is not a top performer in any complex task who has bypassed the 10 years of hard work necessary to reach the top.[2]

At the 2012 London Olympics, Laura Trott, a twenty-year-old from Cheshunt in Hertfordshire, won two gold medals in track cycling. But Laura has acute asthma. When she was born a month prematurely suffering from a collapsed lung, doctors first warned her parents that she might not survive. Then, after she made it to childhood, they advised her parents that she should take up sport in an attempt to regulate and bring her breathing under control. In fact, she only chose cycling because her mother decided to take it up in an attempt to lose weight. But Laura's determination to overcome her health problems, combined with her disciplined approach to the sport she elected to pursue, means that she now has a collection of European, world and Olympic gold medals.

Not bad for an asthmatic!

Winston Churchill once wisely commented: 'Continuous effort not strength or intelligence is the key to unlocking our potential.' Of course, we know this is true. Unfortunately, we also know too many stories of unrealised potential and unfulfilled talent; so many people with so much untapped, unharnessed ability; highly gifted people who somehow have lacked the dedication, commitment or perseverance to capitalise on their head start in life.

Every world-class sprinter, whatever their reputation, knows that a big race is won or lost at the training ground long before it is ever won or lost in the Olympic stadium. To that end, they will train for years for a race that will last a handful of seconds. They take nothing for granted. They know that all athletic success is the result of the slow business of building good skills and habits through disciplined training, persistent practice and huge amounts of sacrifice. They understand more than anyone else that no amount of enthusiasm on the big day, or showboating on the start line, can ever make up for deficiencies in their training and preparation.

Gary Player, the famous South African golfer, won 165 tournaments on six continents over six decades and is widely regarded as one of the greatest players in the history of the game. He tells an interesting story:

> I was practicing in a bunker down in Texas and this good old boy with a big hat stopped to watch. The first shot he saw me hit went in the hole. He said, 'You got 50 bucks if you knock the next one in.' I holed the next one. Then he says, 'You got $100 if you hole the next one.' In it went for three in a row. As he peeled off the bills he said, 'Boy, I've never seen anyone so lucky in my life.' And I shot back, 'Well, the harder I practice, the luckier I get.'[3]

But it is more than practice. Simply playing a lot of golf, soccer or chess is never enough. What's required is a mind-set of never being satisfied with your current ability, a passion to aim just beyond your capability and, most importantly, a never-ending resolve to dust yourself off in the face of defeat and try again. And if there is any grain of truth in the 'You either have it or you don't' philosophy, it is only this. What you either have, or you don't have, is a story that is strong enough, big enough and honest enough to keep motivating you; to believe in yourself, to make you go again, push yourself one more time, take another shot.

This pattern, of course, is not limited to the world of sport. Good musicians, writers, dancers, painters, architects, doctors, engineers, poets and many more, will all tell you the same thing – their art requires enormously hard work and huge levels of perseverance.

Ludwig van Beethoven, the German composer and virtuoso pianist, remains one of the great composers of all time. His story is one of supreme musical achievement – no composer before or since has exerted more influence. And Beethoven's story is also one of extraordinary triumph over tragedy – his hearing began to deteriorate in his late twenties and yet he continued to conduct, perform and even compose some of his greatest work, even after becoming completely deaf.

As a young boy, Beethoven's interest in and aptitude for music was noticed by his father – a musician at the Court of Bonn – who, from that moment on, took it upon himself to tutor and encourage his son in the development of his talent day and night. Responding to this, the young Beethoven showed such promise that by the age of thirteen, in 1783, renowned musician Gottlob Neefe wrote of him: 'If he continues like this he will be, without doubt, the new Mozart.'[4]

But the story of Beethoven's 'genius' is not quite what it has sometimes been portrayed as. In October 2005, the handwritten score of one of Beethoven's most revolutionary works was discovered by a librarian cleaning out a dusty cabinet in a seminary in Pennsylvania, USA. The eighty-page manuscript for a piano version of *Große Fuge* (Great Fugue) dates from the final months of the composer's life. It was an extraordinary find; the historic work had been missing for 115 years since being auctioned in Berlin in 1890.

However, the rediscovery of the document itself was overshadowed by the greater secret it revealed. It gave the world a new insight into Beethoven's methods and led to a whole-scale rethinking of the formerly popular view that the great composer's genius meant he simply heard the unwritten music in his head and then scribbled it down, note perfect, in one go.

The manuscript is written in brown ink, in black ink, in pencil and in red crayon. But, more than that, it includes a huge number of crossings out, corrections and deep multiple rubbings out. Occasionally the paper is even rubbed right through, leaving small holes in it. There are smudged alterations and even several places where the composer has had to paste new pages over the originals, because they have been changed so many times.[5]

Beethoven had often spoken of his slow, painstaking process of writing, tinkering with and perfecting his work. On one occasion, for instance, he confided to a friend: 'I make many changes, and reject and try again until I am satisfied.'[6] But, until 2005, the words of the great maestro were usually dismissed as modesty rather than honesty.

Put another way, if motivation is what gets you started, as Aristotle said, habit is what keeps you going and developing. Skill is not just the result of our genes – instead it emerges through the rigours of disciplined and persistent practice. What separates the mediocre from the good, the good from the very good and the very good from the extraordinary is habitual practice and long-term commitment.

We are creatures who are always in development. Excellence is about the ongoing interaction between our genes and our environment – our experiences and circumstances, our physical and intellectual activity. And it's this mix which produces our unique set of capabilities. We are not trapped. We can channel the direction of our development.

None of this is to imagine that every person has the same resources and opportunities, or that anyone can become great at anything they choose. For all sorts of biological and social reasons some of us start out better equipped than others, whether at football, maths, English, golf, music or whatever. But without doubt, as the number of hours devoted to practice escalates, so the relevance of initial differences melts away.

The key point is this: talent is a process, not a 'given'. Excellence is not hardwired. You have to work at it!

It is no surprise that exactly the same principle applies to the disciplines of our character development and spiritual formation. Far from being a quick-fix, these disciplines require exactly the same sense of focus and intentionality, dedication and self-sacrifice as any other. As Esther de Waal reflects, 'a life without boundaries can never become a life that is constructive, creative and life-giving'.[7]

Since my teenage years I have chosen to follow Jesus – to make him my role model. That means that, the way I see it, if I want to live well, my task is to adopt and constantly work at the kind of habits and disciplines that Jesus had.

It is easy to be tempted to believe that although Jesus looked like an ordinary human, being 'divine' somehow made him invincible; a kind of first-century Superman without the tights! Dealing with the highs and lows, setbacks and struggles, temptations and fears of life was never going to be any problem for him. According to the Bible, however, our stained-glass-window ideas of him don't fit the reality. Jesus was human in the very fullest possible sense; he aged, experienced hunger, thirst, pain, sorrow, tiredness, joy, pressure, tension, rejection, fear, anger and stress – the full gamut of human feelings, needs and emotions. And, the Bible insists, Jesus was tempted in exactly the same way as we are.[8]

So, as Dallas Willard put it, 'We can be very sure that what Jesus found useful for the conduct of his life . . . will also be useful for us.'[9] Jesus' use of solitude, reflection, space, service of others, silence, prayer and the study of scripture, which all had a disciplinary role in his life, are likely to also prove very useful ingredients to sustain me as well.

Who fully understands the interplay of nature and nurture; the interaction between our genetic makeup and our social conditioning? But what we do know is that, in large measure, each one of us becomes the person that we practise being.

12
Learning the Hard Way

It was 20 July 1969. Neil Armstrong, the thirty-eight-year-old commander of *Apollo 11*, who had just become the first human being to set foot on the surface of the moon, delivered his famous line: 'That's one small step for a man, one giant leap for mankind.'[1]

But, unbeknown to the estimated 600 million people worldwide who watched and listened, enthralled by his words, the real drama had taken place several hours earlier in the hazardous minutes leading up to the lunar module's touchdown on the Sea of Tranquillity.

The fact that *Eagle* – *Apollo 11*'s lunar module – successfully landed at all was due in huge measure to Armstrong's extraordinary clarity of thought and his ability to make split-second life-saving decisions. As he later put it, 'In my view, the emotional moment was the landing . . . the business of getting down the ladder to me was much less significant.' And, as he explained in another of the many interviews he gave in the years that followed: 'The landing approach was, by far, the most difficult and challenging part of the flight. Walking on the lunar surface was very interesting, but it was something we looked on as reasonably safe and predictable . . . Pilots take no special joy in walking: pilots like flying. Pilots generally take pride in a good landing, not in getting out of the vehicle.'

With just ten minutes to landing, Armstrong and his co-pilot Edwin 'Buzz' Aldrin stood side by side, space-suited and anchored to the floor of *Eagle* by harnesses, with the task of safely bringing it from a height of 50,000 feet, where it was orbiting at a speed of several thousand miles per hour, down to the surface of the moon, in what amounted to a controlled fall. With no atmosphere, neither wings nor parachutes would have been of any use; the only means of controlling the descent was by varying the thrust of their descent rocket.

Everything had gone according to plan so far, but now the problems started. As the lunar module made its final descent Armstrong noticed that the landmarks he was navigating past were coming up around two seconds ahead of the information *Eagle*'s computer was giving them. As a result he realised that because of the height and speed *Eagle* was travelling at, they were going to overshoot their designated safe landing area – the inviting plain on which their hopes had been pinned.

Meanwhile, as Aldrin cross-checked data from the lunar module's radar with that of the computer, he found a discrepancy of several thousand feet. Because he knew that the radar's information was more reliable, he decided to instruct the computer to accept it. But, as he hit the necessary buttons, the piercing buzz of the master alarm filled *Eagle*'s cabin. The two men looked down and saw the 'PROG' warning light glowing sulphuric amber on the computer display.

'Program alarm,' announced Armstrong, his voice even, but his words urgent. Aldrin instructed the computer to display the alarm code and '1202' flashed onto the screen.

Back at NASA's Mission Control in Houston, Texas, communications with the lunar module were cutting in and out. Information was coming in for a few seconds before headsets were filled with static and computer screens were blanking out again.

And to add to their problems, even when the instruments were functioning, there was a 2.6-second delay in communications with the moon. Those present retell the story of how the seventy or so people in the control room caught their breath in unison at the moment when the *Eagle*'s landing radar abruptly corrected their computer read-out and the little graphic of the lunar module on the screens in front of them suddenly jumped four miles off-range.

Now, with the moon only a thousand feet below the *Eagle*, a new landing site had to be found. Trying to abort the landing at this stage would be neither easy nor certain of success. But as Armstrong looked ahead, he saw a field of boulders, scattered around the dark lip of a crater, into which the computer was blindly flying them.

So, he made a huge decision. He disengaged the computer and took manual control of the craft. Mission Control had little idea what was going on. All they knew was that Armstrong was now on his own, a quarter of a million miles from home, and there was nothing they could do to help.

Staring out of the small window in front of him, Armstrong pitched *Eagle* back and forwards, working hard to avoid fields of giant rocks and boulders. His unnatural calmness masked the fact that the telemetry in his suit was telling Houston that his pulse was now racing at more than 150 beats per minute.

As he edged forward he could see a small clearing bounded by craters. Now, the moon was just a hundred feet beneath them. This had to be the place, but *Eagle* needed to be brought down in a straight vertical line. Any horizontal movement at the point of impact could snap off one of her matchstick legs. As if to make the situation even more dangerous, the descent rocket was whipping up so much dust that it was now impossible to see the surface. Armstrong had no choice but to fly these last moments by instinct.

All the years of preparation, the billions of dollars, the energy, the dedication and the sacrifice of so many was now compressed into the next sixty seconds and the instinctive judgement of one man.

Armstrong wrestled with the controls. *Eagle* was now hanging around twenty feet above the surface of the moon, the point at which bailing out becomes impossible so that if the manoeuvres you make don't work, you crash.

In the end, through all the confusion, *Eagle* settled into the dust so easily that neither Armstrong nor Aldrin even felt the impact. Armstrong's hand flew to the Engine Stop button and he took a breath and announced: 'Shutdown.'

Then there was a moment of stillness. The two men turned to face each other and clasped hands. Armstrong announced to the world: 'Houston. Tranquillity Base here. *Eagle* has landed.'

Armstrong had guided *Eagle* to a graceful touchdown with just twenty seconds of fuel to spare.

How did he do it? What was it that enabled Armstrong to land that lunar module in the face of such incredible odds?

Neil Armstrong was a test pilot. It was once said of him that, 'He flies an airplane like he's wearing it.' Such talent was born of a passion for aviation that had burned within him from his very earliest days combined with thousands of small choices and learnt decisions over many years. He had logged over three thousand hours at the controls of over two hundred aircraft ranging from canvas gliders that only used a dashboard compass for navigation to supersonic experimental jet fighters with gigantic rocket engines grafted onto the fuselage.

During training for the *Apollo 11* mission, Armstrong had landed the lunar landing training vehicle with less than fifteen seconds of fuel left on several occasions. Once, he had even had to eject from it just seconds before it smashed into the ground and exploded.

Thousands of small choices throughout his flying career, each one requiring effort and concentration, meant that when it really mattered, Neil Armstrong had the skill to do what was required of him automatically. It had become second nature.[2]

That's exactly what Aristotle taught about developing skills of character. 'We are what we repeatedly do. Excellence, then, is not an act, but a habit,' he said.

When someone has chosen a thousand times to do something that is good and right, that requires effort and concentration, but that doesn't 'come naturally'. On the thousand and first time, they find that they do what's required automatically; by 'second nature' as we say. On that thousand and first occasion, it really does look as if it 'just happens'; but reflection tells us that it is much more than that.

Our characters are formed as the hard, wise and courageous choices we make slowly, and sometimes painfully, become second nature. This does not happen naturally or by accident. Instead it is born out of the same ongoing self-discipline that's required to do anything in life really well. Character development, like the development of all other skills, is the task of a lifetime.

The route to living well is through the hard work of first identifying and then practising relentlessly the strengths and skills you need in order to turn them into consistent habits. Character is formed by thousands of small choices and learnt decisions over many years, so that when the test comes we do what is required by instinct – by second nature.

For those who fail to cultivate such reflexes and habits, all too often the tough decisions and choices that life throws at them prove to be insoluble. Although none of us is immune from moral struggle, for those who, through discipline, acquire the necessary skills, many of the situations others experience as crises pass them by almost unnoticed. Learning to live well is, like every other discipline, about slowly developing the right instincts and habits as a matter of second nature. Though, to emphasise it again, it is never too late to begin working at developing the character we want to have and be known for.

There is one more essential lesson to learn from Armstrong – one that we neglect or ignore to our cost. Character formation is just like the development of the skills that enabled Neil Armstrong to land *Eagle* safely on the surface of the moon. Armstrong's 'external' physical, mental and coordination skills sprang from his deep, lifelong, internal passion for flying! Only this was powerful enough to fuel, and constantly renew, his commitment to the hard work – often in the face of setback and failure – of developing and honing the skills he needed to achieve his goal.

Our 'outer' achievements are inseparably linked to our 'inner' motivation. Our behavioural skills – and sadly our issues – are always linked to spiritual roots. Just as the foliage of a tree can never be healthy unless it has a strong, deep and healthy root system which gives it life, so we can never achieve, let alone sustain, the development of good character divorced from attention to the inner world of our spirituality.

These two great principles – of the necessity for inner rather than externally imposed motivation, as well as a commitment to self-discipline that, though it springs from the former, still has to be nurtured – were both taught to me through my traumatic childhood experience of attempting to learn to play the piano.

I used to dread Wednesday afternoons. Every week, after school, my mum would walk with me up the hill from our house in South London to my piano lesson. Besides keeping up with my mum, I had to carry my music book in a little brown cloth bag. I hated that bag and I hated the music I had to play from it.

On arrival at Miss Owen's house, I'd sit waiting in her hallway, with my mother, until it was time for the dreaded lesson to begin. It was just like going to the dentist – but far more painful. On being ushered into the front room, I'd sit, perched at the piano, while my mum sat listening in the corner. For an excruciating hour, I'd attempt the impossible – to somehow convince Miss Owen that I'd spent the last seven days practising the piece she'd set me the week before.

It was an agony, for me and for her. The problem was that I hated practising the piano; all those staves and clefs, keys and scales, flats and sharps, chords and octaves. It was too much. I had other ideas about life. I wanted to be free; free to do what I liked; free to play football; free to watch TV; free to mess around; free to do nothing. And especially free not to practise the piano.

Miss Owen used to nag me and remind me regularly that 'playing makes perfect'. Taking a completely different tack, my mum would try to encourage me by sitting down with me at our piano, opening my music book to the required page, stopping to listen to me as I attempted to play a few lines and even wandering away trying to whistle the tune I was playing – an extraordinarily difficult task. But alas, none of this bore fruit. As they say, 'you can lead a horse to water, but you can't make him drink'.

Then, one Wednesday, out of the blue, it all came to a head. As my fingers stumbled clumsily over the keys in another vain attempt to make it through the latest piece Miss Owen had set me, she suddenly began to sob; then, before I knew it, she was crying uncontrollably and had rushed from the room.

That was the last time I ever saw Miss Owen. My mum picked up my music book, put it into my music bag and we left. And I never had to attend another piano lesson again.

But here's my secret. Now, almost half a century later, I wish that I could play the piano. I mean, I wish I could really play the piano. I have to make do with bashing out, in an all-too-mechanic and lumpy style, the same old tune – the only one I ever learnt – 'The Dance of the Tin Soldiers'. Instead, I wish my fingers could dance and skip effortlessly across those keys. I wish I could play like Lang Lang, Elton John, Stevie Wonder, Alfred Brendel, Murray Perahia, Carole King or Gary Barlow. But I can't.

There's a huge difference between someone, like me, who's been given the basic building blocks of reading music and can play, note-by-note, the tune they see written down, and someone who has music deep in their soul; someone who, through the discipline of practice, has reached the point where musical structures and principles are so much part of them that they can play jazz! Players like me are limited to playing exactly the same tune in precisely the same careful way every single time. We have no choice. I do not have the skill, the confidence and the creativity to improvise or to put my own style on a piece of music; I am imprisoned by the basic rules that I was taught. I just don't have the freedom to know how to break them and make music from my soul.

Over the years, every time I hear a great piano player play, and allow myself to dream boyishly that I could do the same, I reflect on those Wednesday afternoon lessons with Miss Owen. And as I do, I realise again, with the benefit of half a century of hindsight, what my problems were.

First, I held the mistaken belief that freedom in life stems from escaping discipline. It took me longer than it should have to realise that far from being the enemy of freedom, discipline is actually its friend and an essential part of the journey towards its fulfilment.[3] But, second, I had no inner drive to play the piano. I now understand that real desire can never be externally imposed, but rather has to be ignited within – and then self-discipline does its job.

Everyone has heard the popular saying: 'Give a man a fish and you will feed him for a day; teach a man to fish and you will feed him for a lifetime.' That same kind of principle applies to the development of all skills and behaviours. Give a person a command for a particular situation, and you help them to live appropriately for that moment, or in other identical situations; give a person an internal story worth living by and they'll develop the self-discipline to be able to navigate situations for which they have had no specific instructions.

13
Get Wired

Some years ago I saw the following anonymous quotation written on a wall in a school:

> *Watch your thoughts, they become words.*
> *Watch your words, they become actions.*
> *Watch your actions, they become habits.*
> *Watch your habits, they become your character.*
> *Watch your character, it becomes your destiny.*

In the film *Evan Almighty*, God decides to give Congressman Evan Baxter a real chance to live up to his campaign slogan, 'Change the World'. He tells Evan that he has to build an ark, just like the one Noah constructed, as there is going to be a huge flood. Though Evan accepts the challenge and builds an ark, the pressures of his task begin to take their toll on his family life. As this tension mounts, in one scene Evan's wife is sitting in a restaurant and calls the waiter over, who just happens to be God in disguise – though, of course, she isn't aware of this fact. He draws her into conversation and she begins to tell him about the ridiculous boat-building scheme that her husband is convinced God has asked him to complete. But, she explains, even that would be OK if only God would answer her prayer for patience! The 'waiter' responds with these words:

> If someone prays for patience, do you think God gives them patience? Or does he give them the opportunity to be patient? If they pray for courage, does God give them courage or does he give them the opportunity to be courageous? If someone prayed for their family to be closer, do you think God zaps them with warm fuzzy feelings? Or does he give them opportunities to love each other?[1]

Our social, moral and spiritual development requires commitment, practice, cooperation, reflection, stickability, humility and self-control – in short, huge ongoing effort. It is only through hundreds and hundreds of hours of practice that those who work at them in this way develop reflexes that eventually become second nature, allowing them to make decisions and choose behaviours that, though they have become obvious or natural to them, are not so to others.

Good ethics are about everyday life – our passions and perceptions – and the slow cultivation of wise virtues and moral habits. These are developed in much the same way as any other skill: kindness, selflessness, hospitality, humility, honesty, gentleness, patience, simplicity, compassion, service and sacrifice all involve time and practice. All of which means that every moment, even the most mundane, is an opportunity for moral formation and development. And the point of all this training and discipline is that when the pressure is on, we do the right things naturally.

Besides anything else, habits save time, which means that we don't have to constantly think about what to do while we are in the middle of doing it. If you had to think hard about tying your shoelaces or setting the table or simple work routines every time you did them, your productivity level would drop like a stone. The ratio between your thinking and doing would be far too top heavy. When what we do becomes routine or second nature, it sets us free.

The great majority of life is spent in preparation, so that's exactly where the emphasis of our character development needs to be. The point of all this is that, on the day that it matters – at the moment of pressure and decision – we have already learnt how to do the right things and make wise responses as a matter of second nature. In a crisis, it is only ever the habits, the instincts and the skills that we've already formed that can help us. So, our task is to consciously choose to practise those habits of behaviour which, though awkward and clumsy at first, will gradually become second nature and, when emergency strikes, we will do by instinct.

There is a story that's told about the Israeli violinist Itzhak Perlman, who contracted polio at the age of four. Ever since, he has had to wear metal braces on his legs and walk with crutches, yet he has become one of the great virtuosi of our time. On one occasion, he came out onto the stage and slowly made his way, on his crutches, to his chair. He sat down and laid out his crutches, in his usual style by his feet, to begin playing. He placed the violin under his chin and began tuning the instrument when, with an audible crack, one of the strings broke. The audience expected him to send for another string but, recognising that this would seriously delay the concert, instead he signalled the conductor to begin, and then proceeded to play the concerto entirely on three strings. At the end of the performance the audience gave him a standing ovation and called on him to speak. What he said, so the story goes, was simply this: 'Our task is to make music with what remains.'[2]

It is only the hard work of developing good values and practices, as we slog life out, that helps us live consistently, stay true to our convictions and become exceptional; making beautiful music, even though faced with the constant challenges and struggles of being human.

I've discovered, to my cost, that not even the greatest of one-off experiences, however inspirational at the time, has the power to transform my character. In the end, only an ongoing commitment to work continuously at being the person you want to be – which itself can only be informed and inspired by the story you've made your own – will make the difference.

To say it again, the 'external' formation of good social and moral habits highlights our dependence on our 'inner' spirituality.[2] It is impossible to divide the two. You'll struggle to get one without the other.

It is a little like piloting a sailboat. We can hoist the sails and steer the rudder but, in the end, we are utterly dependent on the wind. The wind does the work. If the wind doesn't blow – and sometimes it doesn't – we will sit still in the water no matter how frantically we rush around. Our task is to do whatever enables us to catch the wind.

Over the years I have discovered that God is the wind in my sails, without whom I would have long since run out of momentum, direction, stamina and patience. In and of myself I just don't have what it takes to keep going. The Bible, of course, has huge amounts to say about our relationship to God and our dependence on his Spirit, working in us. Paul, in his letter to the followers of Jesus in the city of Philippi, explains that 'it is God who works in you to will and to act in order to fulfil his good purpose'.[3] And to his friends in Corinth he writes: 'As the Spirit of the Lord works within us, we become more and more like him and reflect his glory even more.'[4]

Following Christ is not some bold attempt to bravely get on with life under our own steam as we work *for* God. Instead, the Bible always presents it as working *with* God, by whom we are enabled. To harp back to a previous metaphor, the healthy tree is always dependent on its roots!

In this context, it's worth thinking again about Jesus' exhortation to 'Love God' and 'love your neighbour as yourself'. Interestingly, many more people talk of being committed to the second of Jesus' statements, but of struggling with the first. The two clauses of Jesus' statement, however, are inseparably interwoven – for him it was not a case of 'Here's two: choose your favourite.' Everything hangs 'on these two commandments', he emphasised – they are 'interdependently' true, rather than 'independent' of each other. For me, it is my love for God – and God's love for me – which funds, fuels and sustains me in the frequently challenging and demanding task of deliberately working at loving others, of trying to put their needs first, of being patient and finding new courage. Indeed, even in the struggle of the disorientating times when I am in the doldrums, it is my relationship with God which literally re-inspires me – which fills me again with new hope and direction.[5]

Since the day that I made that decision to follow Jesus – forty-five years ago – it is his story which has been not only my inspiration, but the one which, to this day, continues to motivate, shape and hone the way I see things and the person I want to become. And, to tell you the truth, from the bottom of my heart, I have never heard of a better one.

But the job is never done. There is no finish line, but rather the ongoing task of learning and continuing to grow. So, if I read the text of this book five years from now, I hope that I would want to change, edit and add to it from my greater experience and insight.

I have a repeated conversation, with a succession of different people, mostly in their middle years, who sit down to chat with me – over a drink or a meal – about the future; their future. They tell me of their dreams and hopes. They explain their sense of feeling trapped by their current situation, and of wanting to take a different road through the next stage of life. But, finding themselves so far from where they would like to be, they are not sure of the way forward, nor even if there is a road towards their goal at all.

The good news is that, in my experience, there is always an onwards pathway. 'It is never too late to be what you might have been,' wrote George Eliot. It is true, of course, that the further you are from the road that you now realise you should have chosen earlier, the tougher it is to rejoin it. There are all sorts of reasons for this, from difficult relationships and existing commitments to the ongoing implications of past mistakes, but the best route is always the right route forward.

The time is always right to do what is right. Choosing to live by the story you really believe in, from this moment onwards, always makes more sense than any other option. 'If you can't fly then run, if you can't run then walk, if you can't walk then crawl, but whatever you do you have to keep moving forward,' said Martin Luther King.

A young child gets out of bed and then spends the whole day asking 'why?': 'Why has that man got a bald head?' 'Why do I have to have a sleep?' 'Why do the stars only shine at night?' 'Why do cows moo?' 'Why don't horses moo?' 'Why do birds live in trees?' . . . The questions go on and on; they have no end. We are all born curious.

But then, one day – it might be at the age of eighteen, or twenty, or thirty, or forty-five, or seventy . . . we stop asking questions. We stop being curious. That is the moment when we stop growing. Some people stop growing at a very young age. Some people never stop till the day that they die. Don't plateau. Get out of bed and use every day that God gives you to grow – intellectually, spiritually, emotionally, socially and morally. Be curious! Become the person you were meant to be!

Neuroscientists often use the metaphor of the 'wiring' of the brain, which – though, of course, there are no real wires involved – is a very helpful picture for describing the way in which information is processed within the brain through electrical activity.

The last twenty years or so has witnessed a revolution in neuroscience and therefore our understanding of the human brain.[6] Whereas it used to be believed that our brains were set in early childhood and that long before adulthood we had been neurologically hardwired to perform functions in a particular way, we now know that's not the way it is at all. Our brains are flexible, elastic, constantly changing and capable of growth, always giving us the capacity to develop new qualities, new habits and new abilities throughout our lives.[7]

The habits we cultivate actually change the wiring and size of different sections of our brains, and make these responses automatic. This, by the way, is why, however hard and painful the process of developing a new habit is – like learning to drive a car – there comes that wonderful moment when you suddenly realise that you're now so familiar with what you once didn't know how to do that it has become second nature and you are doing it automatically.

The other day I picked up a magazine with an article in it about the average speed of the four semi-finalists' first service at the US Tennis Open in 2011. Roger Federer – 115 mph, Andy Murray – 113 mph, Novak Djokovic – 112 mph and Rafael Nadal – 110 mph.[8] That is ridiculous! For the vast majority of the human race, even being able to see a ball approaching at such speeds would be an achievement, let alone the skill to read it, move to it, control it and return it, all in the matter of a split second. Experience – lots of the right kind of practice – changes our brains and responses.

Professor Eleanor Maguire from University College London has devoted years to studying the brains of trainee taxi drivers as they learn what is known as 'the Knowledge'. London taxi drivers have to learn 25,000 streets and 20,000 landmarks in order to qualify. Maguire's ground-breaking research has revealed that there is an area of the brain – vital for memory and navigation – which grows in response to a taxi driver's learning.

This part of the brain – the hippocampus – which plays a vital role in storing spatial memories, is much larger in taxi drivers than in the average person in the street, particularly on its right side. And the longer a black-cab driver has been cabbing, the larger their hippocampus has become!

However, when Maguire studied London bus drivers, she discovered that they don't have the same enlarged hippocampus – they only drive restricted routes. But, more than that, only around half of trainee taxi drivers actually pass the Knowledge and it was exactly those that showed the greatest growth of the hippocampus.

Maguire's research shows that the brain behaves just like a muscle. If you use a particular brain region, it grows! Or, in her words, 'experience can change the brain'.

All this research is still at an early stage. Did those taxi drivers who failed to qualify lack a hippocampus that was sufficiently flexible? Is genetic disposition involved? What we do know is that when Maguire's team did further work with ex-cab drivers to see what the impact was when they stopped using their hippocampus 'professionally', they discovered it shrinks back to its normal shape.[9]

When we exercise the muscles in our body, they get stronger, and if we don't use them, they get weaker. Exactly the same is true of our brains. Mentally, morally, socially, spiritually, we get good at what we practise.

If we can develop our brains to memorise countless London street names along with their locations in relationship to one another, or to learn a new language, or to play an instrument or see a very fast-moving tennis ball, what if we can also develop them to help us be more compassionate or less greedy, for example?

What if the first decision, however hard that is to take, to give my time or my money to a local charity creates a new wiring in my brain, which from then on makes it easier to be generous? Or conversely, what if the choice to cheat on my tax return leaves an electronic pathway in the brain which makes it easier to cheat on other things, and people, as well? And suppose the decision to bite my tongue and reflect on the insensitive comment I thought I just heard from a colleague, rather than to jump in with all guns blazing, leaves a pathway which makes it easier to be patient when someone subsequently behaves in a truly offensive manner.

The message is clear – experience will change your brain.

Work hard at getting it 'wired' well!

14

Putting it On

Some years ago I was told the story of two brilliant young Scottish surgeons who had studied together in the 1920s and were the best of friends throughout their college years, as well as close rivals for all the prizes for academic excellence.

The years passed quickly. Two decades later – by which point they had both achieved significant professional recognition – one of them was involved in a complex operation on a patient that went tragically wrong. During the surgery, which lasted several hours, at a critical point in the procedure he asked an assistant for a dose of a particular type of drug. Being handed it in a flask he administered it. It was the wrong one. But it was too late. It proved lethal. The patient died.

The case was emblazoned across the national press and a huge, high-profile court case followed. In the end, though the surgeon was cleared of any wrongdoing, his reputation was in tatters, he retired, moved abroad and sometime later died.

Many years later, at the end of his career, the surgeon's friend and 'rival' gave an interview to a medical magazine, in which he was asked about the old court case and its outcome. He explained that though he stood by his friend because the unfortunate surgeon had been handed the wrong medication and in the intensity of the moment hadn't thought to check whether it was the drug he had called for, in fact things could have been different.

He said that though the two of them were always compared against each other, in truth his friend was far brighter than he. 'But that was his problem,' he added. 'Because his academic brilliance was enough to carry him through – not only his college years, but also his early career – he spent far too many hours on the golf course and not enough of them in the operating theatre watching, assisting and learning from senior professors of medicine. If he'd have given more time to that and less to golf, the patient would have lived.'

He went on to explain how if his friend had 'put the hours in', his experience would have told him that the flask was the wrong weight for the drug he had asked for. He also explained how he would have learnt that, as a failsafe, the wisest surgeon always double-checks the medication as 'second nature'; whatever the pressure of the situation. All this, he said, would have been a matter of instinct and should have happened without even the slightest thought.

It is a strange thing: while we regard the habit of lying, for instance, as a moral outrage, those of inactivity, indifference, negligence or nonchalance are often just accepted as part of a person's character – 'It's just the way he is,' we say. But creating new pathways in the mind – consistent ways of reacting and responding – is a bit like slowly making a new path through the woods: it takes persistence. If you just keep on walking the same route – as if there were a path there already – over time the new path appears. And as long as you keep walking it, it stays.

The British Cycling team won seven out of the ten track cycling gold medals in the London Olympics in 2012, matching their achievement in Beijing, four years earlier in 2008. When interviewed about the reasons for the team's continuing success, Dave Brailsford, their Performance Director, summed up their race-winning philosophy in a fascinating phrase: 'the aggregation of marginal gains'. 'The whole principle', he said, 'came from the idea that if you broke down everything you could think of that goes into riding a bike, and then improved it by 1%, you will get a significant increase when you put them all together.'[1]

Acknowledging that nothing made up for a lack of fitness and conditioning, he insisted that there are multitudes of other small gains that might seem peripheral, but that, taken together, can make all the difference. Disciplines like sleeping in the right position and using the same pillow, even when you are away from home training in different places, so that you're a little bit less tired; always washing your hands thoroughly, without ignoring the bits between your fingers and under your nails, so that you get ill a little bit less often; spraying alcohol on the wheels of the bikes to remove any tiny bits of dirt or oil to improve their traction.

'They're tiny things, but if you clump them together it makes a big difference,' said Brailsford. 'None of them alone will win you the gold medal but, taken together, alongside the huge sacrifices involved in the team's training and racing programme, the attention given to these small gains can add up to a large – potentially race-winning, or record-winning – gain.'

If you have an outstanding maths or English teacher you will, of course, be inspired by them. But, as good as that is, all good skills are both taught as well as caught. Just sitting around a maths classroom in the presence of an inspirational mathematics teacher is never enough. It's essential to engage each student in a deliberate, disciplined and stretching course of study. Only the combination of inspiration and dedication to keep practising will get the result you are looking for.

In just the same way, as we've already seen, moral habits and skills need to be intentionally taught. They will not simply be caught through some strange osmosis as the result of hanging around in the right kind of environment. We need to be far more deliberate than that.

This ancient truth has been understood by those of many different traditions. For instance, as the Buddha explained: 'Farmers [Irrigators] channel the water; fletchers straighten the arrow; carpenters work the timber; the wise tame themselves.'[2]

At the beginning of the sixth century, a young Italian by the name of Benedict of Nursia decided to give up the comfort of his student life in Rome, escape the city and live as a lone hermit in a cave near Subiaco. The problem was that before long he had attracted a large number of followers, with the inevitable result that all sorts of struggles and tensions began to develop within this accidentally formed community.

Learning from his mistakes, Benedict made the decision to begin again and develop an intentional, organised community. And it was out of this experience that he wrote his now famous book *Rule of Life*.[3]

Benedict's book was packed with insights and practical suggestions around how to develop an attitude of mind and a way of life that create the freedom to fulfil Jesus' command to love God and to love others as we love ourselves.[4] It was so good that it is still used today around the world by modern-day Benedictines. He was very clear that it is impossible to learn new ways of living and being without effort. As he put it: 'We cannot attain our highest potential selves without discipline and training.'

To read contemporary terminology back into Benedict's world, his teaching was based around an understanding that – just like IQ – EQ and SQ are also capacities that have to be nurtured and developed.

The character traits we desire need to be chosen through an act of will, and then implemented with determination, even when our emotions or immediate thoughts might be suggesting quite different responses to us. That's how you acquire any skill. It's how you learn a language. It's how you master playing chess. It's how you get fit. It's how you become the person you were meant to be.

Paul, the writer of so many of the letters to early followers of Jesus, had a lot to say about this process. Just as with the conscious decision we make about which clothes to 'put on' when we get up in the morning or when we go out in the evening – casual or smart – so we have to make deliberate choices to 'put on' certain character traits, and to 'put off' others.

> You were taught . . . to *put off* your old self, which is being corrupted by its deceitful desires; to be made new in the attitude of your minds; and to *put on* the new self . . . Therefore each of you must *put off* falsehood and speak truthfully to your neighbour, for we are all members of one body. 'In your anger do not sin': do not let the sun go down while you are still angry . . . Do not let any unwholesome talk come out of your mouths, but only what is helpful for building others up according to their needs, that it may benefit those who listen . . . Get rid of all bitterness, rage and anger, brawling and slander, along with every form of malice. Be kind and compassionate to one another, forgiving each other, just as in Christ God forgave you.[5]

> But now you must also rid yourselves of all such things as these: anger, rage, malice, slander, and filthy language from

> your lips. Do not lie to each other, since you have taken off your old self with its practices and have *put on* the new self, which is being renewed in knowledge in the image of its Creator . . . .Therefore . . . clothe yourselves with compassion, kindness, humility, gentleness and patience. Bear with each other and forgive one another if any of you has a grievance against someone. Forgive as the Lord forgave you. And over all these virtues *put on* love, which binds them all together in perfect unity.[6]

Putting off bad habits and putting on new ones both require the discipline of consciously deciding, again and again, to do certain things in certain ways, in order to embed desired patterns of behaviour deep within the actual physical structure of our brains – just as we learn from contemporary neuroscience.

We often use the phrase 'putting it on' about someone who we think is pretending to be something they are not. It carries the accusation of hypocrisy. The point is, however, that we all have to go through the phase when, if we are going to get anywhere at anything, adopting that action or attitude feels artificial, unnatural and fake. But gradually, bit by bit, the deliberate putting on of these qualities will, in fact, transform our character at its deepest level until they become second nature.

If there are habits to be learnt, there are also those that have to be unlearnt. And, of course, just as it is possible to acquire a skill, it is equally possible to neglect it. You can learn to play the trombone, speak another language, juggle a football or walk a high-wire, and then slowly lose that skill through neglect and lack of practice. In just the same way, kindness, generosity and slowness to anger have to be practised as well as maintained by constant usage.

The goal is slowly to reach the point where we live well, not because of a sense of externally imposed duty, but because the character that has been formed within us has become our second nature; we've slowly learnt to do those things automatically that previously we would have struggled to do at all.

When I was a kid, each summer my parents would take me, along with my brother and two sisters, on regular day trips down to Brighton – the closest beach to South East London – on the train. And, as part of this regular treat, each of us would be bought a stick of Brighton Rock.[7] Famously, you can bite into Brighton Rock wherever you choose; you can chop it up into small 'sweet sized' pieces, or you can suck your way right through it. But whatever you do, the letters are always there. 'Brighton' is what that stick of rock says all the way through.

Character is just like that. It's the pattern of thinking and acting that runs right through someone, so that whenever and wherever you encounter them, and whatever the circumstances that surround them, they are consistent. They have become the genuine thing.

15

A Counter-revolutionary Life

The story is told of how John Howard Yoder, the American theologian and ethicist, best known for his pacifism,[1] was once in public debate with an army general who was the current Chairman of the Joint Chiefs of Staff, the highest-ranking military officer in the United States and principal military advisor to the President of the United States.

The lively exchange moved between the discussion of policy and ethics. Both men argued their respective positions with some passion. However, as the debate closed, the general concluded with these words to Yoder: 'In the end, whatever our differences, we serve the same God.' All would have ended well without Yoder's response: 'Unfortunately, sir, I think not.'

Over the centuries, various lists of virtues have been produced, along with some very sharp disagreement over what they should contain. Thinkers from Homer to David Hume and Benjamin Franklin to Friedrich Nietzsche have all proposed lists which illustrate vividly their differing starting points and goals; between them they name everything from ambition, assertiveness, defiance, detachment, determination, focus and pride to flexibility, generosity, gentleness, humility, loyalty, patience, self-sacrifice and service. It's a confusing and contradictory list – but the nub of the issue is this: your story and its *telos* counts for everything.

Having defined 'well-being' as life's *telos*, Aristotle went on to identify his list of virtues – the ideal character traits – which, for him, would achieve his goal. This consisted of nine intellectual and another nine moral virtues, all developed through study and habit.[2]

And the most important of these, he argued, are *sophia* (wisdom – the culmination of years of learning), which he said sits above all the other virtues, and *megalopsuchia* (magnanimity, benevolence or greatness of soul), which he considered to be 'the crowning virtue' of a great person.

Developing any virtue, Aristotle said, is like learning to hit the bull's-eye, bang in the middle of the target. Vices, on the other hand, are what you get ensnared in when you miss the target either by over- or under-shooting.

So, for example, he suggested that courage (one of his nine moral virtues) is the 'mean' (the bull's-eye) between a vice of excess rashness (too much confidence and too little fear) and a vice of deficiency of cowardice (too little confidence and too much fear). A modern-day example might be defining the mean between a cheapskate and a shopaholic as a responsible spender!

In the same way, Aristotle taught, regarding honour and dishonour – an extremely important topic for the ancient Greeks – that the virtue of magnanimity, benevolence or greatness of soul is the bull's-eye (the mean) between vanity or boastfulness (a vice of excess) and humility or shyness (a vice of deficiency).

For Aristotle, a *megalopsychos* was a man of honour, who refused to be petty; who was willing to face danger and take action for noble purposes; who was prepared to encounter danger and trouble with tranquillity and firmness; who delighted in acts of benevolence; who despised injustice and meanness, and who sacrificed personal ease, interest and safety to accomplish noble tasks. Whatever else you might say about the *megalopsychos*, the magnanimous or great-souled man, he was not humble![3]

It is already pretty clear that Aristotle's brand of well-being was rather exclusive – and only available to the elite few. But he also taught that in order to achieve *megalopsychia*, health was a necessary precondition and that wealth, along with friends, fame and honour, were embellishments – the icing on the cake – which accompany the good life. A bit of a 'health and wealth' champion! Though, for him and his audience, this elitism was never problematic; inequality was popularly believed to be part of the natural order of things and taken for granted by the ancient Greeks.

In the end, it turns out that Aristotle is, rather unsurprisingly, a perfect example of his own teaching. Like he said, it's the story you live in that determines what you believe, and what you believe always shapes who you aspire to become.[4]

Aristotle lived in a world filled with stories of powerful gods and goddesses; immortal giants of incredible strength and stamina who locked in combat for the glory of supremacy. Greek mythology taught that the Titans, a race of primeval deities,[5] were overthrown by a pantheon of younger rival gods, when Zeus the king of the gods, the ruler of Mount Olympus and the ultimate god of power, led his siblings – the Olympians, including Poseidon, Apollo, Aphrodite, Athena, Hades, Hermes and their brothers and sisters – to victory in the War of the Titans.

This then is Aristotle's story; the context of his thinking and writing about virtues and character formation. It's where he gets his role models from. No wonder that he believed what he believed! Both consciously and subconsciously our behaviour is inseparably linked to our beliefs, and in ancient Greek mythology control, supremacy, strength, power, muscle and bite were what mattered. The question is this: what do we believe in? In the end, it always shapes who we become.

Alexander the Great (356–323 BC) was tutored by Aristotle from the age of fourteen to sixteen. From there, he quickly went on to earn himself all-time legendary status as a ruthless warrior by eliminating his rivals, and invading, conquering and crushing any opposing powers with brutal force.

By the age of thirty, undefeated in battle, he had created one of the largest empires of the ancient world. Plutarch, the Greek historian, even said that 'When Alexander saw the breadth of his domain, he wept for there were no more worlds to conquer.'[6]

But, at the age of thirty-two, he was dead and his central goal of unifying and consolidating his newly established empire was in tatters. Worse was to come. In the years following his death, a series of bloody civil wars, led by his surviving generals and heirs, tore his infant empire to shreds.

According to Plutarch, Alexander's genius was in his gift of perception and his ability for cool, penetrating and calculating logic, but, he says, he also possessed a violent temper and a rash, impulsive nature that he never conquered or subdued.

Both consciously and subconsciously our behaviour is shaped by our beliefs. There is, of course, a huge aspirational gap between our desires and our delivery – sometimes the result of woodenness and sometimes of deliberate wickedness. But even this does not invalidate the core principle that our foundational beliefs will find expression, one way or the other, in our reactions and responses, our deeds and our demeanour. Our core values and commitments – which make up the pattern of life we aspire to follow – have consequences for both our attitudes and actions. The story we believe always shapes who we aspire to become.

So, the issue is this. If our morality hinges on the development of some intrinsic virtues, how do we know which ones they should be? And even when we've agreed them, how do we define them?

It's easy to assume that when we use words like 'generosity' or 'inclusion', 'peace' or 'justice', everyone knows what we are talking about – that the definition of these simple and commonly used words is universally agreed. However, each is a big word in need of definition and content. Take 'peace' for instance. What constitutes real peace? When Mahatma Gandhi, the political and spiritual leader of India during the Indian independence movement, spoke of the pursuit of peace, his model – non-violent resistance in the face of injustice – stood in stark contrast to that of many other world leaders, for whom armed conflict had been a well-trodden pathway.

Throughout my life, this has been the challenge of Jesus. His definitions are not just everybody's definitions with a little 'flavour of God' thrown in. After all, why would he have been crucified simply for reinforcing what everyone else already knew and believed? It's sobering to remember that Pilate permitted the killing of Jesus in order to secure peace and justice – Roman style – in Judea.

The story which has inspired me and which gives Oasis a sense of ongoing purpose is that of Christ's life and example; his teaching, his analysis of humanity, his death and resurrection. It is the pursuit of Jesus which shapes all our definitions and continues to inspire and inform our future vision.

The contrast between the world of Aristotle and Jesus' example could not be greater, more profound or more pronounced. Rather than teaching control Jesus demonstrated self-control;

rather than pride, humility; rather than power, servanthood. For him, far from representing various shortfalls or deficiencies, these qualities sat at the very heart of his whole approach to freedom and fulfilment.

Jesus taught us to behave as if nothing we give away could ever make us poorer, because we can never run out of what we give. Rather than trying to grip your life with tight, anxious hands, unclench that fist. Open your hand. Don't plot and scheme about tomorrow. Live with reckless generosity. Serve others. Give up the best seat. If you try to keep what you have, you'll lose even that. Give it away, and you'll get back more than you bargain for. Give it away, and you'll get back more than you ever dreamt you could get.

This is a way of being human which nobody had ever imagined before. And it poses a huge question that none of us can ignore. What is success?

The concept of 'Level 5 Leadership' was developed by Jim Collins, a business consultant who, in the late 1990s, explored how companies can make the transition from 'average' to 'great' and why some fail to do that. He argued that the key ingredient that allows any organisation to become great is that it is led by someone who has the skill to blend extreme personal humility with intense professional will.[7]

Good to Great, the book in which he set these ideas out, was seen as a countercultural manifesto and went on to become a massive bestseller, reaching an audience far wider than the traditional corporate community and transforming the way that many thought about business leadership.[8]

However, Collins' whole approach is firmly focused around the 'bottom line'. And the bottom line for any company is profit. How do you develop a company that is successful in terms of its financial performance over a sustained period? Collins' view of 'greatness' and 'success' is defined by this ultimate goal. In the end, 'being humble' is a means to an end; a route to success; a tactic designed to drive up your share price.

But here's the really counterintuitive, countercultural thought. What if humility is the end itself? What if this is the way to life whatever the outcome – the way to become the person you were meant to be? 'Follow me,' said Jesus.

Friedrich Nietzsche, the German philosopher, who began his career studying Greek and Roman literary texts, noticed precisely these differences between Christian morality and Aristotelian ethics, but saw Aristotle's elitism as a great strength. In his view, the Church, alongside Judaism, was responsible for the development of what he termed 'slave morality', which he claimed had turned poverty, humility and meekness into virtues in an attempt to exalt their own low place in society.[9]

As far as Aristotle, Nietzsche and countless others are concerned, Jesus' thinking was 'upside down'. Jesus' response, of course, is simply this: he came to turn the status quo the right way up! Or, to put it in the words of G. K. Chesterton, 'The

Christian ideal has not been tried and found wanting. It has been found difficult; and left untried.'[10]

This remains the challenge of Jesus' life and message: you win looking like you are losing.

16

A Different Kind of Vision

The New Testament writers know all about Aristotle and the ethics of ancient Greece.

They agree with Aristotle that rule keeping doesn't work; they understand that character development is the only way. But that's where they part company. Aristotle might be right about his approach to ethical thinking but, as far as they are concerned, his content – drawn from Greek mythology – is way off beam. It's sending him in completely the wrong direction. Jesus' values were not just a repackaging of everyone else's, with a little bit of extra 'Christian' flavouring thrown in to spice them up. Jesus' values were far from 'common sense' – and they were unique and radically different from anything else on offer.

So, it is no surprise that when writing to the followers of Christ who live in Galatia, Paul writes: 'But the fruit of the Spirit is love, joy, peace, forbearance, kindness, goodness, faithfulness, gentleness and self-control. Against such things there is no law.'[1]

Count the number of moral virtues Paul lists. It is nine!

Who is Paul's model for this set of virtues? Zeus, Poseidon, Apollo, Athena, Hades, Hermes or one of the other Titans? Beyond the slightest doubt, this is a description of Jesus.

Where does Paul's list start? Not with *sophia* (wisdom), but with unconditional, self-giving love.[2]

Where does his list end? Not with the benevolent control of others, but with self-control.

Paul knows that Jesus subverts Aristotle's approach. Which is why, when writing to the followers of Christ in the city of Corinth, he says:

> Where is the wise person? Where is the teacher of the law? Where is the philosopher of this age? . . . Jews demand signs and Greeks look for wisdom [*sophia*], but we preach Christ crucified: a stumbling-block to Jews and foolishness to Gentiles, but to those whom God has called, both Jews and Greeks, Christ the power of God and the wisdom [*sophia*] of God.

And if that is not plain enough, he adds: 'For the foolishness of God is wiser than human wisdom [*sophia*], and the weakness of God is stronger than human strength.'[3]

Paul's point is clear: if it doesn't look like Jesus, you've bought into the wrong story and the wrong set of virtues.

So it is that in the same letter to his friends in Corinth, Paul goes on to pen the famous words:

> If I speak in the tongues of men or of angels, but do not have love, I am only a resounding gong or a clanging cymbal. If I have the gift of prophecy and can fathom all mysteries and all knowledge, and if I have a faith that can move mountains, but do not have love, I am nothing. If I give all I possess to the poor and give over my body to hardship that I may boast, but do not have love, I gain nothing.
>
> Love is patient, love is kind. It does not envy, it does not boast, it is not proud. It does not dishonour others, it is not self-seeking, it is not easily angered, it keeps no record of wrongs. Love does not delight in evil but rejoices with the truth. It always protects, always trusts, always hopes, always perseveres.
>
> Love never fails . . . where there is knowledge, it will pass away . . .
>
> And now these three remain: faith, hope and love. But the greatest of these is love.[4]

And, equally, it is why another New Testament writer, Peter, quotes an old Hebrew song when talking about Jesus' life and example: 'The stone the builders rejected has become the chief cornerstone.'[5]

In 1843 London's Trafalgar Square was opened during the reign of King William IV. The four enormous corner plinths were built around the centrepiece of Nelson's Column to hold statues of George IV, William IV and two heroes of the British Raj – Sir Henry Havelock and General Sir Charles James Napier. However, William died shortly before its completion and, having failed to provide the funds for his own statue, his plinth was to stand empty for the next 156 years.

In order to mark the Millennium, the two thousandth anniversary of Jesus' birth, it was decided that an appropriate statue should, at last, be installed on the vacant plinth. But the big question was: of whom should it be? Suggestions ranging from Queen Victoria to Winston Churchill and Florence Nightingale to William Shakespeare were put forward for consideration. In the end, a statue of Jesus was temporarily installed. However, rather than calming the debate, this solution simply intensified it.

Cast in synthetic resin and white marble dust, *Ecce Homo* was installed in July 1999. Mark Wallinger's life-size statue was a mere fraction of the size of the plinth itself. Naked except for a loin cloth, with his hands tied behind his back and a gold-plated barbed-wire 'crown of thorns' on his bald head, Jesus looked tiny and inconsequential by comparison with the grand scale of the rest of the square. Most passers-by were amazed by the image – it was so totally different from the usual, triumphalist images of Christ that adorn buildings and famous works of art. Where, people asked, were his beard, his long hair, his halo, his fine robes? And why was he so tiny and vulnerable?

Many objected strongly. As one man commented: 'You couldn't put your faith in someone like that; he's as weak as a kitten.'

But perhaps the most intriguing comment came from one of the UK's leading Christian magazines: 'He looks so vulnerable, so frail, an anomaly, half-naked, weak. Will it send out all the wrong signals?'

That always was the scandal of Jesus. If you are looking for a boot-wearing, power-mongering, swashbuckling god, look elsewhere.

Jesus' project is a project for turning the world upside down and inside out; for re-humanising human beings. To help us see things another way. To bring us a different vision of life and of God. To find a different story. One worth living by.

But tragically, people still believe that the Christian God is a God of power, law, judgement, hell-fire and damnation. A God whose strapline is something like, 'Get in line fast or I'll squash you!'

Jürgen Moltmann, a German born in 1926, became a prisoner of war in the Second World War. During this time he became a Christian. In 1972 he published his classic book, *The Crucified God*. In it he makes an extraordinary statement: 'A God who cannot suffer is poorer than any human. For a God who is incapable of suffering is a being who cannot be involved. Suffering and injustice do not affect him . . . so in the end he is also a loveless being.'[6]

In declaring himself to be love, God is stating his commitment to involvement with the world he has created. He is wearing his vulnerability on his sleeve. As C. S. Lewis recognised, 'Love anything and your heart will certainly be wrung and possibly be broken.'[7] To love is to suffer and the greater the love the greater the suffering.

The press sometimes talk of a new government 'coming to power'. Our politicians speak of being 'in power'. Government ministers refer to 'having power'. But actually the term 'minister' means 'servant'. I am currently the 'senior minister' of Oasis Church, Waterloo – which is another way of saying that I am its 'primary servant'. Ministers are not 'in power' – they are always 'in service'. To call a person to the office of 'prime' minister is simply another way of indicating that this person is the 'chief' public servant. The late Czech president Václav Havel put it this way: 'Genuine politics – politics worthy of the name – the only politics I am willing to devote myself to – is simply a matter of serving those around us: serving the community and serving those who will come after us. Its deepest roots are moral because it is a responsibility expressed through action, to and for the whole.'[8]

Far from being impoverished by our service, however, it turns out that we are infinitely enriched by it. This truth is reflected in the lyrics of the song of the early Christians that Paul quotes in his letter to the infant church in Philippi, in which he encourages his friends there that, in their relationships with one another, they should aim to develop the same mindset as Christ Jesus:

Who, being in very nature God,
did not consider equality with God something to be used to his
own advantage;

rather, he made himself nothing
by taking the very nature of a servant,
being made in human likeness.
And being found in appearance as a man,
he humbled himself
by becoming obedient to death –
even death on a cross!

Therefore God exalted him to the highest place
and gave him the name that is above every name . . .[9]

These words express the core identity of Jesus – they explain that his servanthood was not a step away from his true nature; not some kind of temporary interruption of his true character. Rather, in the humble Christ we finally encounter the God of the universe exactly as he actually is.

Self giving is not the same as selflessness. Most, but not all, acts or attitudes have some element of self-interest built into them. Selfishness is the exclusion of others, self-interest is the recognition of the need to 'love your neighbour as yourself'. A healthy sense of self-worth, self-esteem and self-interest are all traits of an emotionally stable and balanced and generous individual.

Even the briefest reading of the Gospels quickly confirms that far from urging his followers to act like apathetic doormats, Jesus, in his teaching about loving enemies, counselled active, creative and strong responses to aggression that maintain our self-worth without resorting to violence.

The idea of a 'meek and mild', 'wouldn't say boo to a goose' Jesus is far from the reality of the picture that the Bible paints. Whatever he was, Jesus was never passive. Take, for instance, his famous statement: 'If anyone slaps you on the right cheek, turn to them the other cheek also.'[10]

If we are honest, this particular piece of advice seems absolutely ridiculous to most of us. Why should we let someone openly abuse us in this way without fighting back? What we miss is that Jesus' words would have sounded very different to his oppressed and downtrodden first-century audience. Whether they were for or against him, not one of them would have failed to appreciate just how radical, active and downright confrontational this teaching was.

It was part of the culture of Jesus' day that a 'superior' would often inflict a backhand slap on an 'inferior', not so much to injure as to offer insult, humiliate and degrade them. Masters would backhand their slaves, husbands would backhand their wives, adults would backhand children and Romans would backhand Jews. But this kind of blow was only ever administered to 'subordinates'. Equals fought using their fists and forehands, the backhand was designed to be a stinging sign of disdain. Strong cultural taboos, however, also meant that the person hitting out would never use their left hand. This was kept for 'unclean' tasks, and carried a taboo that overrode all other concerns.[11]

So, by teaching his lowly hearers to turn the other cheek, Jesus was suggesting a little act of defiance. Rather than suggesting that they deal with the insult offered by 'lying down' to take some more, the reverse is true. He was teaching his listeners to quite literally stand up for themselves. By following Jesus' advice to turn the other cheek, they would make it impossible for their abuser to inflict another blow using the back of their hand. The taboo on using one's left hand meant that the aggressor had only one option if they wanted to continue to hit out. They would have to slap or punch their victim using a forehand blow – which is precisely the point Jesus is making.

Turning the other cheek wasn't passive; it was proactive. Through it, the 'inferior' was making a powerful statement: 'I'm a human being, just like you. I refuse to be humiliated any longer. I am your equal. If you want to hit me again you are going to have to acknowledge that fact.' Far from advocating a weak and weedy 'just take it' mentality, Jesus is encouraging exactly the reverse: 'Stand up for yourself, take control, but don't answer your oppressor on their terms.'

Jesus' way was neither cowardly submission nor violent reprisal. It was non-violent, but definitely not non-resistant. It involved bold, energetic and even highly costly confrontation.

The point of all this was not to enshrine this particular action as the only way of responding to his teaching for all time. Jesus' example was just that: an illustration. His challenge to us today is to continue to think and act imaginatively and creatively; constantly finding new ideas for rejecting passivity, resisting evil and asserting our dignity, but doing so non-violently.

Over the last century, world leaders like Mahatma Gandhi, Martin Luther King Jr and, in his later years, Nelson Mandela have all taken Jesus' 'upside down' non-violent ethical approach to life seriously, as each has tried to think of creative, surprising ways of practising the 'turn the other cheek' principle as an alternative to the tactics of power and aggression in order to achieve their goals.

The story of Gandhi – who never held political office or military command and yet led the people of India to freedom – is a powerful testament that a real and solid commitment to non-violence can achieve massive social change and the liberation of oppressed people.

But equally astonishing is that, rather than finding inspiration for his stand in his own Hindu faith, Gandhi self-consciously based his ideas on the teachings of Jesus. The story is told of how Rev. Charlie Andrews, a young Christian minister who was to become a lifelong friend to Gandhi, heard of his work and travelled to meet him. Within minutes of their first meeting Andrews came face to face with the hatred and abuse that Gandhi had to put up with every day. A white gang start shouting abuse at Gandhi and Andrews as they walked down the street. Andrews was rather concerned about the very real possibility of being attacked and suggested that perhaps he and Gandhi turn around. But Gandhi was not intimidated.

'Doesn't the New Testament say, "If your enemy strikes you on the right cheek offer him your left"?' Andrews was rather bemused by Gandhi's sudden desire to quote Bible verses. 'I think perhaps the phrase was used metaphorically,' he responded.

'I am not so sure,' Gandhi countered. 'I have thought about it a great deal and I suspect Jesus meant that you must show courage. Be willing to take a blow, several blows, to show you will not strike back nor will you be turned aside. And when you do that, it calls on something in human nature; something that makes his hatred for you decrease and his respect increase. I think Jesus grasped that and I have seen it work.'

Even today, despite the fact that there is almost universal admiration and respect for leaders such as Gandhi, Martin Luther King and Mandela, the myth that violence is the only solution to many of the world's problems still thrives. Jesus' words, 'Love your enemies', probably amount to, at one and the same time, the most admired and least practised piece of teaching in history.

More often than not, Jesus' advice about non-violence is viewed as a kind of impractical idealism. Extraordinarily, however, no such charge is ever made against violence, in spite of the fact that history has proved, time and again, that war and hostility solves nothing in the long run. Despite thousands of years of individual, tribal and international bloodshed, the last century has produced the most horrific wars ever seen. All we do know is that whenever aggression is met with aggression the beast of violence is fed and grows stronger. 'Whoever opts for revenge', says the Chinese proverb, 'should dig two graves.' Or as Jesus put it, 'all who draw the sword will die by the sword'.[12]

As the world struggles to find a way out of the chaos resulting from the doctrine of 'might is right' and 'he who has the biggest guns wins', those who make Jesus their model are called to live out their commitment to the ethic of non-violence or 'assertive meekness' demonstrated by Christ.

The example of Jesus is my guiding story: it frames my life – it gives me direction and purpose. Though I am broken and there remains a huge gap between my aspiration and my performance, the invitation to join in with the unfolding story of the establishing of the kingdom of God – an ecosystem of justice, inclusion, grace and hope – continues to both inspire and shape me.

17
The Indelible Image

What is it that makes a human human?

The Creation of Adam by Michelangelo – the image of the near-touching fingers of God and Adam, part of the fresco he painted on the ceiling of the Sistine Chapel in Rome – has become one of the single most iconic images of humanity and has been reproduced in countless imitations and parodies.

God's right arm is outstretched to impart the spark of life from his finger into that of Adam. Adam's left arm is extended in a pose that mirrors God's – a reminder that humanity is created in the image and likeness of God. Adam's finger and God's finger are not actually touching, which creates the impression that God, the giver of life, is reaching out to Adam and Adam is receiving.

The *Oxford Dictionary* chooses to define a human being as 'a man, woman, or child of the species *Homo sapiens*, distinguished from other animals by superior mental development, power of articulate speech, and upright stance'. It defines *Homo sapiens* as 'the primate species to which modern humans belong'.[1] But the Bible's story of humanity transcends this and is built on the key statement, which Michelangelo seeks to illustrate, contained on its very first page:

> *So God created mankind in his own image,*
> *in the image of God he created them;*
> *male and female he created them.*[2]

So, in the end, for all those who choose this story, the challenge of answering life's biggest question 'Who am I?' is inextricably linked to that of grappling with what it means to be made 'in the image of God'.

The fact that Genesis 1 simply uses the term 'image of God' and then fails to unpack its meaning is, in itself, a real clue. It's clear that its writer has made a big assumption – the assumption that the phrase didn't need explaining. This can only be because it made plain and obvious sense to its original audience.[3] So, what was it that was so clear to the first readers of Genesis but which is lost on us today?

Though often misread as a scientific textbook, Genesis 1 is actually a poem – and one of a whole number of creation stories that were circulating around the ancient world in the first and second millennium BC.[4] And central to them all was an idea that was common across the Ancient Near East; a human being could be the dwelling place of a god and, as a result, function as an image of that deity. But, of course, the most likely candidate to fill this most important of roles in any society was the king who, in the creation story of his culture, was regularly regarded as the life-long incarnation of the local god.[5]

All of the societies surrounding Israel were hierarchically structured. At the top of the social ladder sat the king, who, as we've just seen, was believed to be the representative of the local god. Just below him came the priests, and below them the bureaucrats, the merchants and the military; while at the very bottom came women, peasants and slaves. By this clever device, the poor were oppressed and the social order was given religious legitimisation.[6]

So here comes the bombshell. The writer of Genesis 1 goes out of their way to deliberately undermine the popular belief of the time that it was only the monarch who was the divine representative. To the contrary, they boldly declare that the whole of humankind enjoys that privilege, as well as the responsibility that goes with it. And if oppression on the basis of class or ethnicity is dealt a blow through this revolutionary statement, so is its cousin: sexism. Genesis 1 insists that both male and female together are created, side by side, in God's image. The language of the author is as deliberate as it is subversive.

The image of God is universalised. Not just the king; not even just the nobility or the priests; but every man, every woman and every child bears God's image. We all have the honour and the responsibility of being God's representatives on earth.[7] There are no exceptions and there is no hierarchy!

Not only was this view of women unique among the cultures of the time; it still presents a huge challenge to our modern age. In a world still laden with oppressive hierarchy and dictatorship, which all too often sees ordinary people as the pawns of the powerful, the words of Genesis 1 are just as revolutionary today as they were when first penned.[8]

Genesis 1 was written as an attack on the oppressive errors of the popular creation stories of the surrounding cultures.[9] It tells a different story – a magnificent story. There is only one God, he is good and each one of us represents him.

Genesis 1 was never written as a scientific account of 'how' God created the world, but is rather a poetic story explaining the 'why' and 'who' behind it all. It is not about how the world came into being but about why. So, not only does it sit happily side by side with our modern understanding of the science of the first few seconds and subsequent development of the universe – it complements it, adding richness and removing the coldness of a universe filled with matter but devoid of meaning.[10]

To some who see science and faith in opposing corners, it comes as a bit of a shock to learn that the idea that the universe came into being in an enormous explosion of energy, which we know as the 'Big Bang' – somewhere around 13.7 billion years ago – was first put forward in the 1920s by Georges Lemaître, a Belgian Catholic priest! But as Albert Einstein – the world's most famous physicist – himself noted: 'Science without religion is lame; religion without science is blind.'[11]

By itself, the Big Bang theory doesn't tell us how to live. For that we need, not just a cosmology, but a theology. Though scientific rationality may be the key in the battle to understanding the material basis of our existence, there are important questions that science cannot answer – not because we haven't figured them out yet (there are obviously lots of those), but because they are not scientific questions at all; they are questions of meaning.

The new atheists noisily ask why we imagine that such questions are important; for them the universe is a beautiful but cold reality, built on the principle of cause and effect, comprised of matter and anti-matter. 'The universe that we observe has precisely the properties we should expect if there is, at bottom, no design, no purpose, no evil and no good, nothing but blind, pitiless indifference,' Richard Dawkins, the Oxford professor, wrote.[12] However, most of us want to shout back that these questions – the questions of meaning, purpose, belonging and direction – are the most important questions of all. They provide us with the story that we live in!

According to Genesis all human beings are stamped with the image of the Creator, which defines human life as more than merely biological. This means that when we stand before another person, however destitute, disabled, diseased or degraded, we stand before a representative of the divine.[13]

My wife Cornelia has an eye for colour and style. When we first set up the original Oasis housing project for vulnerable and homeless young people in Peckham, South London,

Cornelia spent a great deal of time choosing artwork for its corridors and dining room, for which we also bought a large TV set. But within three weeks of its opening, the halls and dining room were bare. Everything had been stolen by our own residents, working in league with their friends.

We were shocked. Why had those we aimed to help, let us – and more importantly themselves – down in this way?

It took us a long time to realise the depth of emotional and psychological damage that had been done to our residents by the time they came to stay with us. The lack of love, security, nurture and discipline they had endured had taken its toll. The fact that those they should have been able to trust had abandoned, rejected, betrayed and abused them had left them crippled.

We slowly woke up to the fact that whenever we met a person with a severe physical disability, we intuitively understood that their capacity to respond, in a physical sense, in the same way as an able-bodied person was, to one degree or another, limited. But when we encountered someone who had been severely emotionally neglected and disabled, in our naivety we were not ready to compensate in the same way.

The separate story – that of Adam and Eve – contained in Genesis 2 and 3, paints a vivid picture of the moral 'fall' of humanity; our de-humanising through the arrogant pursuit of self-centred ambition.[14] Yet, even so, the biblical account insists that the image of God is not lost.[15] However worn out or distorted, the image of God is indelible; part of each and every person. However far we have wandered from God, we continue to bear his imprint in our lives. St Augustine put it like this, 'we may be sure . . . the image always remains, whether it be so faded that scarcely anything of it is left, whether it be obscured and defaced, or clear and fair'.[16]

We do well to never stray far from this great truth. God, in his generous love, defines and identifies all humanity as made in his image. There is no life that does not deserve respect and is not worth defending with zeal and conviction. Perhaps we can even measure a society's degree of civilisation by the amount of effort and vigilance it imposes on itself out of pure respect for life.

This is where inclusion starts. With the simple but profound truth: 'God loves you whoever you are, whatever you've done, however scarred you are by your past mistakes, wrongdoing or behaviour – God, the God of the universe, made you in his image!'

And once this revolutionary understanding of God – that his first impulse for humanity, all humanity, is outrageous love – is grasped, it shapes not only our message and our work, but us. We recognise that our task, as God's image bearers, is to act as angled mirrors – to reflect God's goodness on earth – and we slowly learn to react and respond with that same love, albeit a limited and broken replica of the real thing.

Our vision becomes one of building healthy inclusive communities that understand and respect the dignity of difference –

where everyone is included and given the opportunity of reaching their God-given potential, regardless of their gender, their marital status, their race, their ethnicity, their religion, age, sexual orientation, social status or physical and intellectual ability.[17]

The famous Danish philosopher Søren Kierkegaard once attended a very grand state service held in the huge cathedral in Copenhagen. All around him were the richest and most powerful people in the land: noblemen, captains of industry, the well-bred, the well-fed and the well-read; the cream of society.

Eventually the bishop began to address the congregation, preaching a sermon from the Magnificat – the song that Mary, the mother of Jesus, sang when she heard she was pregnant.

> *My soul glorifies the Lord*
> *and my spirit rejoices in God my Saviour,*
> *for he has been mindful*
> *of the humble state of his servant.*
> *From now on all generations will call me blessed . . .*
> *he has scattered those who are proud in their inmost thoughts.*
> *He has brought down rulers from their thrones*
> *but has lifted up the humble.*
> *He has filled the hungry with good things*
> *but has sent the rich away empty.*[18]

As Kierkegaard listened he looked around the cathedral at the people draped in ermine robes and dripping with gold and diamonds, and cried. He cried, he said, because he couldn't understand why nobody was laughing.

It is wisely said that you can judge the character of any society by the care it extends to those who are most vulnerable; the character of any person by the compassion they extend to those from whom they have nothing to gain.

I have a friend called Stephen. He is a barrister who defends criminals – his clients are terrorists, murderers, armed robbers, international drug traffickers, city fraudsters and money launderers. When he started out, it was smackhead shoplifters, street dealers, prostitutes in punch-ups and pub glassings.

Some years ago he wrote to me about his experience of defending them:

> The story of one of my 'killer' clients is indicative of nearly all.
>
> His mother was a young black crack addict who raised him in the 90's amidst her own battles – a few days of trying to be a good mum, then back on the game to pay for what went into her veins; the father, a white man, who still lived locally and dealt drugs in a half-hearted way refusing to acknowledge the son, even though they lived on the same estate.
>
> At 14, the son makes a more formal approach to his father. 'F*** off you black bastard' is the paternal response. The killer-to-be loses his grandmother, the one good influence, who dies in his teens. On a diet of chips and

booze he still develops a good height and physique. He is compelling to women and he runs a variety of girlfriends. In his late teens, he determines to be the Big Man locally.

For him, that vision entails getting his own car and heaps of bling. He does not have the capacity for greater vision even as a criminal. He starts to deal, successfully at first, with cocaine and cannabis. He still watches his mother and won't do smack. He starts to consume his own product. Then heroin like his mum. Gear makes him unstable and he slaps his main girl. She too is addicted. A child arrives; then another. He has a lot of other crack women but always returns to her. He loves her.

He hears his own bulk dealer further up the chain wants to enforce the debt he owes – a debt he can't pay. He borrows a gun in drink. In a crack rage, he kills the other man. He wakes up in a jail house with a head that only works to hurt and a body panging cold turkey.

After a month of meeting his solicitor, he and I meet for the first time. Ask me, can I see the image of God in him? My heartfelt answer is resounding. Yes, yes . . . and yes!

Now, on remand he is dry and clean. Unaddled by 'class A' drugs for the first time since puberty.

My first yes is because, whether spoken directly or not, he has deep remorse, not just for himself – and perhaps not for the man that he shot and half buried – but for the mother who never cared for him; for the girls he treated so badly and for the children he may now not see for 25 years. In his pain for these others, the image of God is clear in him. He interrupts our prison conferences to talk about them. They come to him at night.

My second yes is for the distance between where his life is today and where it could have been if he had sought to live it – or if he had half a chance to live it. Hence, I have found there is a sense that it is often when the biblical promise of life abundant is at its most remote that the image of God is most visible.

And yes again – for the goodness that I found in him as the months of preparation for trial move on. The eyes that change from when we first meet – deepening in a way. The casual discovery from a prison psychiatric assessment report that he is a prison 'listener' who is called out of his cell at night to try and talk to other troubled souls in a prison Samaritan capacity; in the decency he shows to me – against a background of being raised amongst folk who would feel no compassion for him.

He, like all of us, can step into or out of God's image; but only to a degree. In our origins and in its potential for redemption, God's image overarches us all.[19]

What is it to be human? It is to be made in the image of the God of love!

18

The Elephant in the Room

If all this is true, there's a big question that we can't ignore any longer.

If the narrative of the Bible – the centre point of which is the story of Jesus and the breaking in of the kingdom of God – is the way of love, joy, peace, forbearance, kindness, goodness, faithfulness, gentleness and self-control, then what about all the brutality, violence and discrimination that are also found there?

How does the Old Testament view of God's decidedly violent and vengeful bouts of behaviour relate to the teaching and attitude of Jesus who, through both his words and example, challenges us to love our enemies rather than to exterminate them?

The story is told of Winston Churchill's son Randolph, who served with his father's old regiment in the Second World War in the Libyan desert and then in Yugoslavia. Holed up in a cave there, with only a Bible to read, he waded through the Old Testament stories of plague, violence and genocide. In the end, utterly overwhelmed by its contents, Randolph came to a clear conclusion: 'What a shit God is!'[1]

Through the centuries, we have to face it, various bits of the Bible have been used to justify some of the most inhumane, brutal and repressive episodes in human history: to sanction crusades, inquisitions and the torture of hundreds of thousands of those of other faiths; to denounce Copernicus's and Galileo's breakthrough in understanding of the cosmos; to approve witch-hunts across Europe and North America, which saw tens of thousands of innocent women slaughtered in the name of God; to portray African people as cursed by God and therefore to justify the enslavement of millions; to legitimise apartheid and anti-Semitism. And still today, to condone the death penalty, to keep women subservient to men, to incite Islamophobia, to insist on a 'young earth' – anti-scientific – six-day understanding of creation, to oppress gay people and to abuse the environment. All these have been 'faith-based initiatives'. A fairly extraordinary record for a tome which is often referred to as 'The Good Book'.

Yet, running counter to all of this, it also turns out that many of the world-changing people we most admire have been inspired by the Bible to live out that upside-down vision of reality: Florence Nightingale, William Wilberforce, William Booth, Anthony Ashley Cooper (Lord Shaftesbury), Martin Luther King Jr, Mother Teresa, Nelson Mandela, Desmond Tutu . . . to name but a few.

Not so long ago I heard someone try to answer this question by suggesting that sometime after the Old Testament was written, God must have gone on a cosmic anger-management course to deal with his impulsive and unpredictable nature. By the time he re-emerged, at the beginning of the New Testament, he'd been rehabilitated into the graceful and loving character that we discover through Jesus.

A rather humorous answer to what is, in reality, a far more complex question!

If the claim that God is love holds any water, then why does the Old Testament contain so much material that, on the face of it, depicts him as fierce, wrathful, violent and vengeful? Why does it so often report him as supportive of a justice system filled with oppressive and discriminatory measures? And what about the various rounds of brutal genocide and ethnic cleansing that it tells us were initiated at his command?

The problem is not just about the brutality and violence of the Old Testament, however. There's some pretty oppressive and discriminatory teaching that – on occasions – also raises its head in the New Testament. What about the fact, for instance, that a straightforward reading of parts of the New Testament has been used for the promotion of slavery and the repression of women, the rejection of gay people and the exclusion and persecution of people of other faiths?

God's relationship with the Children of Israel took place in the messy and often brutal reality of their day-to-day life in the Ancient Near East. To put things in context, although there are no exact dates, scholars place Abraham's life sometime around 2000 BC in the Middle-Bronze Age, and Moses towards its end – still some thirteen hundred years before the birth of Christ – just before the transition to the new technology of the Iron Age took hold.[2]

Here, war and unrestrained violence were commonplace. Here, every nation boasted a god of power to defend their cause and justify their cruel acts of aggression and revenge. It was practically impossible for Israel not to get caught up in the same mind-set. The very fact that she claimed her God was the one true God implied, according to her worldview, that he must be the most powerful god of all. So, when she went to war against her enemies, the expectation was that her God, the Lord Almighty, would demonstrate his power, destroy the opposing armies and, in doing so, vindicate his own name as well as Israel's belief in him.

That's why, if we focus in on individual Old Testament verses and stories, it's easy to fall into the trap of seeing God as a vengeful despot. It is only when we step back, and focus on the overall direction of Israel's relationship and journey with God, that the bigger picture – the bigger story – becomes clear. Only as we do this, do we grasp God's struggle to communicate his love, not just for Israel, but for the whole human race, which was to culminate eventually in the arrival of Jesus – though whom, at long last, we see God's true character and nature without any distortion for the first time.

So why is it recorded that God orders Israel: 'Now go, attack the Amalekites and totally destroy all that belongs to them. Do not spare them; put to death men and women, children and infants, cattle and sheep, camels and donkeys'?[3] Because that's the way people thought in those days. Why is it suggested that God declares in Leviticus 21:16–23 that no man with any physical disability can 'desecrate my sanctuary' by his presence? Because that's the way people thought in those days.

Put bluntly, the reason we find some of these primitive stories of the Old Testament so shocking, violent and brutal is simply because they *are* shocking, violent and brutal. And if we didn't regard these stories in this way, there would be something wrong with our own moral compass.

However, there are two very important caveats to all this.

First, at the very same time, these biblical authors – 'inspired' by their encounter with God – are being challenged and therefore are confronting their society. Through their ongoing journey and dialogue with God they are constantly having to face up to new and better ways of being human – to ideas of mercy, justice, equality, peace, compassion and grace. God is slowly stretching their moral imagination. What about, for instance, God's repeated command that Israel should not deprive the foreigner, the fatherless or the widow of justice?[4] What about God's radical guidance on the ownership of land designed to favour the poor? 'The land must not be sold permanently, because the land is mine and you reside in my land as foreigners and strangers.'[5] Or what of God's determination that no Israelite should charge interest on loans made to other Israelites?[6]

Second, while we are repulsed by the Old Testament's violent stories (because we believe that we are more enlightened), it is sobering to remember that our society is still deeply morally compromised. Have we reached moral maturity yet? Does our society model equality? Is justice freely available to the poor in the twenty-first century? What about the banking system, land ownership and immigration in our globalised world? Is there peace on earth? Does anyone still declare war in the name of their national values and gods? Perhaps we still have further to go than we might think.

As you read through the Old Testament you just can't miss the drip, drip of the slowly dawning realisation that it is the record of how the one true God slowly leads the people of Israel away from their misshapen and distorted tribal ideas about the divine, themselves, their role in the world, as he introduces them to himself, a different way of living and a better way of being human. And, as the story progresses, even the stubborn Children of Israel, with all their preconceived prejudices and cultural blinkers, slowly begin to see that, as the psalmists often had cause to write, 'The Lord is compassionate and merciful. . .and filled with unfailing love.'[7]

Even if only viewed as an anthropological text – a record of the development of human society and moral consciousness – (though as this chapter will explain, I believe it is very much more than that), the books of the Old Testament make for an extraordinary read.

If you ever get a chance to visit the Louvre museum in Paris, head past Leonardo da Vinci's *Mona Lisa*, and don't leave without seeing 'The Code of Hammurabi', which dates back to about 1772 BC. Hammurabi was the sixth king of Babylon, lived around five hundred years before Moses, and is famous as a law giver. Hammurabi's Code is one of the first written codes of law in recorded history. Inscribed in the Akkadian language, it stands over two metres high. The punishments it sets out are very harsh by modern standards, with many offences resulting in death or disfigurement. They are saturated in the philosophy of retaliation. Here is an example:

> If a man destroy the eye of another man, they shall destroy his eye. If one break a man's bone, they shall break his bone. If one destroy the eye of a freeman or break the bone of a freeman he shall pay one mana of silver. If one destroy the eye of a man's slave or break a bone of a man's slave he shall pay one-half his price. If a man knock out a tooth of a man of his own rank, they shall knock out his tooth. If one knock out a tooth of a freeman, he shall pay one-third mana of silver.[8]

Now, for anyone who has read the Old Testament, all this sounds very familiar, except that, in the Law of Moses, it reads: 'But if there is serious injury, you are to take life for life, eye for eye, tooth for tooth, hand for hand, foot for foot, burn for burn, wound for wound, bruise for bruise.'[9]

Moses has taken a giant moral step forward. The Code of Hammurabi is hierarchical. A Babylonian citizen's eyes and teeth are worth more than those of a freeman, which, in turn, are worth more than those of a slave. What Moses does, for the first time in history – as far as we know – is to create equality. An offence against a slave is to be treated as seriously as one against the highest in society.

For all its advances, however, Moses' Law is still based around the same old principle of retaliation, and just like Hammurabi's Code, although it limits this – a tooth for a tooth and nothing more, rather than a man's life for one of your family's teeth! – it still teaches it.

But then comes Jesus!

'You have heard that it was said, "Eye for eye, and tooth for tooth." But I tell you, do not resist an evil person. If anyone slaps you on the right cheek, turn to them the other cheek also.'[10]

The rule book is torn up in Jesus' 'upside down' approach to life.

The philosophy of retaliation is binned.

It is finally clear that God's association with the vengeance and violence of the Old Testament era was never a true expression of who he was so much as the result of his determination to stay involved with his people and guide them to a better way of being human. It is this very desire that, at times, meant he was implicated in, indeed even written up as the architect of, Israel's excessive acts of violence and genocide. The Bible writers put words into God's mouth; the problem is that lots of them stuck.

Finally, however, the penny has dropped. 'In the past God spoke to our ancestors through the prophets at many times and in various ways, but in these last days he has spoken to us by his Son . . . the radiance of God's glory and the exact representation of his being,' says one New Testament writer.[11]

At last!

19

The Sacred Library

So far so good – but the problem is that all this simply poses another, even bigger, set of questions.

What does it mean if we say that the Bible is inspired by God? Is it really the Word of God, or just the collected opinions of a random group of subjective human authors? Can we really have confidence in it? If so, on what basis? Can we rely on it? Can we rely on *all* of it? Does it paint an accurate picture of God? Can we use it as a reliable moral guide on which to build a story worth living by?[1]

For me, the answer to all these questions is a resounding yes. The Bible remains, for me, the most inspiring text that I have ever read; its message has changed, and is constantly challenging and changing my life. The problem is that many more people have read – or tried to read – the Bible than have been given the tools to understand it, with the result that, at best, they find it confusing and, at worst, some of it intolerant and violent.

As a young Christian I was utterly confused, not only by the huge questions around the brutality, oppressive teaching and punitive legislation contained in some parts of the Bible, but also by the fact that no one ever seemed to acknowledge that there was a problem. As a result, I concluded that I must be the only one who didn't get it. I was convinced that I was slow. The answers must, I assumed, be so obvious to everyone else that it wasn't even worth the conversation.

Then, in my early twenties, I went to theological college, where I was sure that these issues would be dealt with thoroughly. So when my lecturers said nothing, and, just to rub it in, none of the other students seemed to be bothered either, once again I concluded that the problem was mine.

And that was the pattern. Over the years, as I left college, became an assistant church leader, then set up Oasis, I always assumed that someone else, somewhere else, far sharper and more senior than I, must have all this sorted.

But as the years went by, I slowly woke up to the realisation that I didn't want to live my whole life with my head in the theological sand. So eventually I began to grapple with the Bible and these huge questions for myself, alongside many others, who I found were thinking around these same issues. What follows, therefore, is something of how, over time, I've come to understand all this, in a quest born not out of any disregard for the Bible's authority, but rather as a way of grappling with it and attempting to take it – all of it, in its entirety, including the unpalatable bits – very seriously.

The idea that the entire text of the Bible was dictated to its human authors, by God and without error or contradiction, is, in my understanding, ridiculous.[2] The writers of the Bible did not take direct dictation from God. Instead, it is clear that their personalities, politics, social understandings and cultural settings all play a part in their thinking and writing. The Bible is a collection of human books written by fallible men whose work bears the hallmarks of the limitations and preconceptions of the times and cultures they lived in.[3]

The writers of the New Testament, however, alongside countless other authors and thinkers after them, are all agreed: through Jesus, for the first time in history, we finally get to see God exactly as he is. God's character is at last, fully, accurately and completely revealed by him. Or, to put it the other way round: if it doesn't look like Jesus, it's not God.

Jesus, however, even as he claimed to be committed to bringing the full meaning of the Old Testament to the surface – 'Do not think that I have come to abolish the Law or the Prophets; I have not come to abolish them but to fulfil them' – is famous for his numerous challenges to its actual text.[4]

'You have heard it said that . . . But I tell you that . . .' Jesus used this well-known formula first to quote from the Old Testament law and then to radically reinterpret (or, to be blunt, in some cases rewrite) it. Indeed, it was his deliberately renegade attitude to these and many other Old Testament laws and teachings that increasingly got under the skin of Israel's religious teachers. They just didn't like the way he chose to ignore their time-honoured interpretations. As far as they were concerned, Jesus' views, along with his whole way of life, were blasphemous and heretical. And as a result, they wanted him silenced.[5]

The fascinating encounter between Jesus and a Jewish mob who had brought a woman to him who they claimed had been caught in the act of adultery is another example of Jesus' perceived heretical approach to Jewish scripture. 'In the Law [a term for the first five books of the Bible] Moses commanded us to stone such women. . . what do you say?'[6] The Pharisees – the guys with a lot more RQ than SQ or EQ[7] – were looking for Jesus to agree with them that the passage from the Old Testament which they were referring to was universally applicable. He did not!

Then there is Jesus' attitude to all those Old Testament Sabbath laws.

In one Old Testament story it is God who commands a rather unsure Moses to execute a man who has been discovered gathering wood in the desert – presumably to use for lighting a fire for warmth or cooking – on the Sabbath day, which was against their Sabbath law.[8] This was based on the fourth commandment:

> Remember the Sabbath day by keeping it holy. Six days you shall labour and do all your work, but the seventh day is a sabbath to the Lord your God. On it you shall not do any work, neither you, nor your son or daughter, nor your male or female servant, nor your animals, nor any foreigner residing in your towns.[9]

Although the writer of the book of Numbers records the man's execution as God's will, Jesus, once again, has a completely different take, not to mention a rather dismissive view of this understanding of God.

> One Sabbath Jesus was going through the cornfields, and as his disciples walked along, they began to pick some ears of corn. The Pharisees said to him, 'Look, why are they doing what is unlawful on the Sabbath?' He answered, 'Have you never read what David did when he and his companions were hungry and in need? In the days of Abiathar the high priest, he entered the house of God and ate the consecrated bread, which is lawful only for priests to eat. And he also gave some to his companions.' Then he said to them, 'The Sabbath was made for man, not man for the Sabbath.'[10]

The Sabbath is not a straitjacket; it is designed to set you free, not to cripple you. The principle of Sabbath is vital. In Egypt the Children of Israel worked seven days a week as brick-making slaves. There was no rest, no moment of recreation under this de-humanising regime. But God rescued them from servitude. He got them out of Egypt and set them free. Now though, the task was to get the old ways and habits of Egypt out of them, because, as these stories show, they had the recurring habit of turning their liberation back into new forms of legalism!

Was Jesus rejecting bits of the Bible? No, he was doing something quite different. He was dismissing immature, over-simplified and legalistic understandings and applications of its ancient text. For Jesus, it was clear that the whole Old Testament is a slowly developing narrative which at times presents some very distorted and juvenile views of God's true nature. Its text, however, in its entirety – including all its most unpalatable bits – is a vital record of the slow journey of the people, whose story it recounts, away from a culture of violence and tribalism, towards an ever-increasing grasp of the true nature of the God who is love. And as they are prompted and provoked by God's interaction with them, slowly their moral consciousness develops. God is love – he always has been, he does not change or evolve: copy him, Jesus taught. Love your neighbour and draw that circle so wide that it includes your enemies![11]

So, how do we read the Bible – the whole Bible – authentically, honestly and consistently?

The Bible charts God's journey with Israel in particular and the human race in general, on whom he will not give up, as he slowly moves them out of and away from the pagan and ill-shapen ideas about him and themselves that, at times, they cling to so desperately. The books that comprise the biblical text form a giant commentary on what God has done in history, from the perspective of its writers and compilers, but also on the constantly developing moral understanding of those who seek to follow him as they move through time.

It is a very common error, but hugely misleading, to think of the Bible as 'a book'.[12] The Bible is actually a library. In fact, the word 'Bible' literally means 'the books'. It is a complex collection of historical documents, written over the course of at least one and a half thousand years and representing various styles, worldviews, languages, cultures, opinions and agendas. As such, it contains numerous, sometimes harmonious and sometimes discordant, even contradictory human voices and perspectives.

The Bible is the account of the ancient sacred dialogue which is initiated, inspired and guided by God with and among humanity. It is with this understanding that the scriptures have to be read, interpreted and acted upon.

The Bible is a conversation that contributes to the gradually growing picture of the character of God; fully revealed only in Jesus. But it is also a conversation that, rather than ending with the finalisation of the canon, continues beyond it.[13] The Bible does not provide the final answer to a whole number of moral issues with which society has subsequently wrestled.[14]

However, ultimately Christianity is not about a book, but about a person, Jesus, who is the full revelation of God – as a number of the biblical writers themselves make absolutely clear. Therefore, we are called to live with the example, character and teaching of Christ as our guide and our primary lens not only for all our biblical interpretation, but also as the basis for our whole way of doing life.

This is how, for instance, William Wilberforce and his friends, all committed followers of Christ, came to the view that slavery was wrong, even though some of the verses of the Bible – the actual words in black and white – clearly have a different view.[15] The Old Testament not only endorses slave keeping and trading, but sets out terms and conditions for its practice.[16] Although the New Testament proposes a more humane form of slave keeping, and no longer supports slave trading, it fails to deliver a clear-cut protest against it.[17]

What guided Wilberforce and his friends, however, was their view of the proper understanding of the nature of the Bible. They did not believe that the Bible was produced by its writers taking blind dictation from God. Instead, they could see that the authors' personalities and cultural and social setting, as well as their understanding of God, all played a part in the formation of their writings.

Rather than basing their approach to slavery, therefore, on the wording of isolated verses or texts, Wilberforce and the abolitionists built their stance around what they understood to be the deeper resonance of the direction of the journey of the whole of the biblical narrative. This was centred on the example of Jesus, who was their compass for this recalibration and who, through his inclusion of both women and various other socially unacceptable groups of his day, challenged social norms and perceived orthodoxy.

God speaks to humanity in countless ways: through friends, music, poetry, film, theatre, sculpture, paintings, dance and even silence, as well as through other literature – religious texts, spiritual writings, popular novels, magazine articles and letters. God's inspiration is everywhere for those who will stop long enough to listen.

The Bible, however, through which we learn not only about the life of Jesus, but – from the Old Testament – about the deeper context of his mission and – from the New Testament – about his ongoing power to inspire and transform our lives, has a unique place in Christian spirituality. It remains today what it has always been: the irreplaceable, central resource for all who seek to understand the shape and content of Christ-centred character formation and spiritual development, built around a love for God that fuels a love for our neighbours and even has the power to include our enemies!

The Bible continues to inspire countless millions of individuals and whole societies. It continues to inspire me towards a better vision of both who I am and who I can become.

20

Thirty Pieces of Silver

'The real voyage of discovery consists not in seeing new sights, but in looking with new eyes,' wrote French novelist Marcel Proust.[1]

Getting our way of seeing – our way of thinking about life – clear is an enormous challenge, but when it is not done, the impact on us and consequences for others can be enormous.

One of the Bible's most famous, and famously difficult, stories is that of the betrayal of Jesus to his enemies by Judas Iscariot – a member of his closest circle of friends. Over the centuries, Judas's central role in Jesus' arrest and crucifixion has not only made him one of the most universally despised characters in all history, but has seen his name become synonymous with betrayal, treachery, duplicity and backstabbing.

Behind the backs of Jesus' other followers, Judas – as we read in Matthew's Gospel – organised a high-level meeting with the religious leaders of Jerusalem to cut a deal. Both sides knew exactly what they wanted, as well as what they were willing to give to get it. Thirty pieces of silver were exchanged – and Jesus' fate was sealed.[2]

The way that the story is told is filled with difficult and unanswered questions. But hidden in the story of Jesus and Judas, though long lost through layers of misreading, misunderstanding and poor teaching, is an important key to understanding the heart of the tension between, on the one hand, the way Aristotle framed the goal of life and, on the other, Jesus' revolutionary vision of being human.

According to the way the story is usually taught, someone had to fulfil the terrible, but essential, task of betraying Jesus. Without a betrayer, Jesus would not have died on the cross. Without a betrayer, a holy God would not have had his wrath satisfied. Without a betrayer, the possibility of forgiveness would have disappeared and humanity would have remained under God's judgement forever. So, where would we have been without Judas?

All this is complicated even further by the popularly held, though in my view nonsensical, belief that God predestines or preordains all history. By this misguided logic, it would follow that, by some terrible twist of fate, Judas had no choice but to become the betrayer of Jesus. For him, this was his inescapable, God-given, predetermined destiny.

I remember listening to Judas's story as a child and being appalled. How could God treat him in this way? And if so much rested on Judas's action, then why didn't the Church credit him for the vital role he played, and the enormous price he paid, in helping to bring us forgiveness? If God required Jesus' death in order to get his moral books balanced, and Judas was the man who delivered it, then surely he should be heralded by the Church and the Bible as a saint rather than finding himself condemned by both?

To add yet another layer of confusion to an already twisted tale, Matthew's Gospel explains that 'When Judas . . . saw that Jesus had been condemned, he was seized with remorse.' It then explains that he attempted to undo the damage he had caused by returning the thirty pieces of silver to the Jewish leaders and declaring Jesus' innocence. Finally, overwhelmed by regret for what he had done and being unable to secure the release of his friend, he left the money with the priests, rushed out and committed suicide.[3]

Why did Judas betray the friend that he had given up his life, family and friends to follow and serve for three years? Why did he then regret, so instantly and completely, what he had done? What was it that was going through his head? If he had slowly come to resent Jesus over those years, why hadn't he just abandoned him and returned home to his easier and former life? If Judas's betrayal of Jesus was such a cold and calculated act, why isn't the glimpse that we get of him in the biblical story filled with words of defiance and a smug smile? If he really despised Jesus, then why was he so remorseful about the outcome of his decision?

None of it makes any sense!

As I've grappled with this story, I've slowly come to see that the real reason we don't understand Judas's actions is because of the misguided way in which we've thought about why it was that Jesus died on the cross.

Jesus' death – his public execution on a cross – represents the ultimate outworking of his teaching, and his teaching is unambiguous. Turn the other cheek. Love your enemy. Do good to those that persecute you. Reciprocal violence is a vicious and deadly downward spiral. Vengeance always leads to reprisal. Once installed within a community such practices become self-perpetuating. Be the place where violence ends.

Judas's actions were not born out of his rejection of Jesus, but rather were a disastrous consequence of his deeply rooted misunderstanding of Jesus' mission – which he shared with many of Jesus' other followers.

On an earlier occasion, Peter, another of the disciples, when prompted by Jesus' question, 'Who do you say that I am?' was quick off the mark with his answer. 'You are the Messiah,' he boldly announced. Jesus' response was to confirm the accuracy of Peter's response but then to go straight on to explain that he 'must go to Jerusalem and suffer . . . and be killed'.

None of this fitted with Peter's ideas about the role of a Messiah, and his instant retort was, 'Never . . . this shall never happen to you!' But Jesus was clear: 'you do not have in mind the concerns of God, but merely human concerns,' he explains. Then he added, 'Whoever wants to be my disciple must deny themselves and take up their cross and follow me.'[4]

Although Jesus identified himself as the 'Messiah', he refused to accept the definition of the term that many of his contemporaries, including at least a significant group of his own disciples, clung to. As far as they were concerned, the Messiah's task was to free them, and the rest of their people, by force, from their enemies. The long-awaited Messiah's task was to lead a violent uprising against the oppressive hand of the brutal Roman occupation and, by that means, to liberate Israel.[5]

Far from not believing in Jesus, Judas was completely committed to him – he was convinced that he was the Messiah: God's anointed liberator of Israel. He had given up his former livelihood to follow Jesus simply because he saw in him a different future for the Jewish people. But, just like the other disciples, he'd never actually grasped that Jesus' mission was to play out his messianic role in a very different, non-violent, way; he had never really understood that Jesus' intention was to bring real peace to all by showing them a different way of living, responding and reacting to the world around them.

The week leading up to the terrible events that put Jesus on the cross began very differently. Jesus had finally arrived in Jerusalem escorted by his disciples, to mass acclaim:

> A very large crowd spread their cloaks on the road, while others cut branches from the trees and spread them on the

road. The crowds that went ahead of him and those that followed shouted:

'Hosanna to the Son of David!'
'Blessed is he who comes in the name of the Lord!'
'Hosanna in the highest heaven!'[6]

The cry 'Hosanna' is a Hebrew word that meant 'save' or 'help'. And the palm branches that the people spread in front of Jesus are also significant. In one of their popular folk stories, which looked forward to the victorious end of their ongoing struggle for freedom from occupation, palms were mentioned as a sign of the coming of the promised liberator (the Messiah).[7] These two symbols alone, set alongside the cry 'Blessed is he who comes in the name of the Lord!', demonstrate that the crowds saw in Jesus the fulfilment of their hopes for political freedom. He was, they dared to believe, the one who would liberate them from Gentile rule, establish peace and drive out the hated Romans. This wasn't the first time that a crowd had wanted to make Jesus their king,[8] but this time he was being recognised as such in the city of their greatest king – David.

If the tension and expectations around Jesus had been growing, they were just about to take an even more dramatic turn. Having arrived very publicly, and to huge popular acclaim, in Jerusalem, Jesus marched straight to the Temple and drove out every last one of the 'get-rich-quick' merchants who did business there. He overturned the tables of the cheating money changers as well as the benches of those selling doves who were in league with the ruling class and were exploiting their own downtrodden people. 'It is written,' Jesus cried at the top of his voice, '"My house will be called a house of prayer", but you are making it "a den of robbers".'[9]

As far as Judas was concerned, Jesus was now riding the very crest of a tidal wave of popularity. The moment was his. The people would have followed him anywhere. He'd entered Jerusalem, the capital city and the seat of the Roman occupation, to mass support and reclaimed the Temple, the most sacred symbol of Jewish nationalism. Now all that remained was to march on Herod's palace, complete the coup d'état, signal that the time had come to take up arms and provoke the ensuing civil war.

But, instead of all this, Matthew reports that even as children in the Temple continued the cry 'Hosanna to the Son of David', 'he left them and went out of the city to Bethany, where he spent the night'.[10]

Judas's head must have been exploding with questions. Did Jesus not see that this was his moment? Was he blind to the mass support he had generated from the ordinary people? Had he lost his nerve? Why did he still lack the confidence to push things all the way? Was there anything that could be done to 'nudge' him in the right direction?

So it was that Judas decided that the only option was to take things into his own hands. He would give his friend the little shove that he needed. He would engineer a showdown and prod his hero into action. And, what is more, the plan he was hatching was failsafe. Why? Because he was convinced that Jesus was the Messiah, which meant he couldn't die. His destiny was to shed the blood of others, not to have his own blood shed. The ancient scriptures foretold it. Therefore, selling Jesus to the authorities was a safe bet. It would force Jesus' hand, the wheel of history would be turned, the people of Israel would be liberated and the world would be changed.

So, as Matthew tells us, Judas 'went to the chief priests and asked, "What are you willing to give me if I deliver him over to you?" So they counted out for him thirty pieces of silver. From then on Judas watched for an opportunity to hand him over.'[11]

Matthew's riveting account of the way that events unfold marches relentlessly on. He now explains that Jesus went with his disciples to Gethsemane – a garden on the hillside just outside the city. Once there, Jesus asked his friends to keep watch for him, while he moved a little way beyond them to pray. But they were tired and on the three separate occasions that Jesus returned he found them all asleep! Finally he confronted them, 'Are you still sleeping and resting? Look, the hour has come, and the Son of Man is delivered into the hands of sinners. Rise! Let us go! Here comes my betrayer!'[12]

Matthew tells us that Judas arrived while Jesus was still speaking.

> With him was a large crowd armed with swords and clubs, sent from the chief priests and the elders of the people. Now

the betrayer had arranged a signal with them: 'The one I kiss is the man; arrest him.' Going at once to Jesus, Judas said, 'Greetings, Rabbi!' and kissed him.

Jesus replied, 'Do what you came for, friend.'

Then the men stepped forward, seized Jesus and arrested him. With that, one of Jesus' companions reached for his sword, drew it out and struck the servant of the high priest, cutting off his ear.

'Put your sword back in its place,' Jesus said to him, 'for all who draw the sword will die by the sword.'[13]

Sadly, Matthew comments, as Jesus was arrested, 'all the disciples deserted him and fled'.[14]

It was early the next morning, Matthew tells us, that the chief priest and leaders of the people came to the decision to put Jesus to death, binding him and leading him away to be handed over to the Romans.

Only now does Judas come to his senses. He finally realises that he has got it all wrong. Jesus will not, even under the greatest provocation, instigate an armed uprising. So he attempts to retract his deal. But, in despair, understanding that things have gone too far and that he now has no power over the inevitable process, he grasps the enormity of what he has done. Through his misunderstanding of Jesus' intentions he has unwittingly brought about his friend's downfall. He can't withdraw his actions, but he can't live with them either. Overcome with remorse, he rushes out and kills himself.[15]

It is a tragic story. But there is one final dimension to this extraordinary tale.

Judas had shared some of Jesus' most intimate moments; he was one of the inner community of twelve. For anyone looking in from the outside, his relationship with Jesus would have appeared, superficially at least, extremely close. Scratch beneath the surface, however, and you discover that Judas was heading away from Jesus and the virtues, values and habits he taught, rather than towards him. But even though he was travelling in the wrong direction, none of the Gospel writers even hints that he was at any time ever held at arm's length by Jesus. It seems that Jesus deliberately left the door of friendship open for Judas as long as possible.

Even at the last moment, extraordinarily, Jesus chose to wash his betrayer's feet and then to share a meal with him rather than to reject him. Perhaps this was just one last-ditch attempt at character formation; one final shot at demonstrating a different way to live, a better way of being human.

Perhaps it was one last chance to whisper into his friend's ear, 'Wake up!'

21

The Table of Friendship

Two Italian scenes.

Scene one: Pompeii, the famous ancient Roman city near modern Naples. Here, on 24 August AD 79, shortly after midday, Mount Vesuvius suddenly erupted in savage violence. Over the next few hours the city – along with its twenty thousand or so inhabitants – was buried, although not destroyed, under a deep layer of red-hot volcanic ash.[1]

Forgotten for more than a millennium, over the last three centuries Pompeii has been substantially excavated, now making it possible to walk its streets again and to visit the sites of many of its original buildings, still standing two thousand years later. Amongst these are various temples, including those of the gods Venus, Jupiter, Apollo, Isis and others.

At the heart of each of these sites sits a high altar, designed specifically for daily sacrifice to appease its all-too-easy-to-anger deity, as well as to win and maintain that deity's favour. But perhaps one of the most striking observations is just how remarkably similar these altars are to those found in countless church buildings today.

Scene two: The Convent of Santa Maria delle Grazie, in Milan. Here, on the wall of the dining hall, hangs one of the most famous, most studied, most scrutinised, most copied and most satirised paintings in the world. *The Last Supper*, by Leonardo da Vinci, represents the scene at the meal Jesus chose to eat with his closest friends on the night before his crucifixion, and depicts the moment he announced that one of them would betray him.

The remembering of this last supper has become central to the practice of the Church around the world, through what is variously known as the eucharist, mass, communion, Lord's supper or the breaking of bread. But why has this event become so important and what does it tell us about the big story we are invited to be part of?

Mark, one of Jesus' first followers, tells the original story of the supper that Jesus had with his disciples hours before he was to be arrested and sentenced to death, noting that:

> While they were eating, Jesus took bread, and when he had given thanks, he broke it and gave it to his disciples, saying, 'Take it; this is my body.'
>
> Then he took a cup, and when he had given thanks, he gave it to them, and they all drank from it.
>
> 'This is my blood of the covenant, which is poured out for

many,' he said to them. 'Truly I tell you, I will not drink again from the fruit of the vine until that day when I drink it new in the kingdom of God.'

When they had sung a hymn, they went out to the Mount of Olives.[2]

Back to Pompeii and Milan. Though we rarely, if ever, stop to think about it, these two very powerful images – the altar and the table – are both used, in different traditions, in the remembrance of the communion service – and they can send very different messages.

Is the eucharist set in the context of a table? Is it based on the original table where Jesus sat to eat one last meal with his followers and served them with bread and wine; the table at which Jesus purposely chose to include Peter who would, before the night was out, deny any knowledge of him and Judas, who was already minded to betray him? If so, it becomes a place of welcome and acceptance for all; a means, and a symbol, of inclusion and reconciliation, of community, of a circle of friends.

Or is the eucharist set in the context of a latter-day altar? If so, its imagery is based, in part, around recalling – or at least referencing – the place where the anger of the appropriate god was pacified by the offering of blood sacrifice.[3]

Perhaps the answer is found in another story told about the same meal?

John's Gospel doesn't record the story of the eucharist at all. Where Matthew, Mark and Luke – the three other Gospel writers – explain how Jesus shared the supper with his disciples just before he was betrayed, John's focus is on a different aspect of the evening's events, which took place just before it:

> It was just before the Passover Feast . . . The evening meal was being served, and the devil had already prompted Judas Iscariot, son of Simon, to betray Jesus. Jesus knew that the Father had put all things under his power, and that he had come from God and was returning to God; so he got up from the meal, took off his outer clothing, and wrapped a towel around his waist. After that, he poured water into a basin and began to wash his disciples' feet, drying them with the towel that was wrapped around him.[4]

Jesus and his friends had gathered for the Passover meal (the greatest of the annual Jewish feasts – which remembered their escape from slavery in ancient Egypt that had taken place over a millennium beforehand and is still celebrated around the world today). At this meal it was customary to have the dust of the street washed from your feet before the celebration got underway. In the first-century world, this was the work of the most lowly slave – at the very bottom of the Jewish social ladder – but because Jesus had asked his disciples to hire a room for the celebration, no such servant was available.

So there they sat, feet caked in dirt, waiting. Waiting until Jesus broke the awkward silence. By choosing to wash his own apprentices' feet, Jesus inverted the traditional, time-honoured values of his culture.

But even as he did so, he also went on to lay a huge challenge at those same feet and – by extension – at the feet of every one of us who chooses to join his story.

> 'Do you understand what I have done for you?' he asked them. 'You call me "Teacher" and "Lord", and rightly so, for that is what I am. Now that I, your Lord and Teacher, have washed your feet, you also should wash one another's feet. I have set you an example that you should do as I have done for you. I tell you the truth, no servant is greater than his master, nor is a messenger greater than the one who sent him. Now that you know these things, you will be blessed if you do them . . .'[5]

Service is never a soft option. Learning to wash the feet of others, whether we regard Jesus' words as literal, metaphorical or both, demands a humility and servant-heartedness that is rarely found in any society or community.

There's a popular myth that serving turns you soft; that it robs you of your self-respect and reduces you to being some kind of doormat; that it is the product of weakness. But far from turning those who choose Christ's way into pushovers who disregard their self-worth, learning the art and discipline of serving transforms and empowers them.

The more we give of ourselves – in genuine love of God and of others – the more we become our true selves. It turns out it is the person who lacks self-esteem who finds it hardest to serve others, to put others' interests first. Self-centred behaviour – a lack of generosity – is a symptom of insecurity, a hallmark of a lack of self-esteem. Selfishness is the outworking of self-doubt. The ability to serve is born not of weakness, but of inner strength.

Jesus once commented, speaking of himself, that 'the Son of Man did not come to be served, but to serve, and to give his life as a ransom for many'.[6] I am convinced that he was speaking of the pattern of his whole life – his approach to each and every single day – his ongoing commitment to the generous service of others which eventually cost him even his life.

The communion table is just that: a table. It is not a latter-day altar. There is nothing that needs to be done to appease a hostile God. Instead, through Jesus' life and character, God has self-revealed as inherently gracious and kind, forgiving and reconciling. God, we discover, is love; not hostile or vengeful, angry or distant. God does not need to be appeased.

In churches where the imagery of the altar rather than of a table has been retained, its symbolism is now intended to speak of a different kind of sacrifice made to a different kind of God than those of ancient Pompeii. Week by week, countless millions of people – young and old – kneel in front of an altar, not out of fear but out of thankfulness, both to receive communion and to offer their lives – their stories – to the God of love as an active expression of sacrifice.

The root meaning of the word 'sacrifice' is 'sacred gift'. Jesus is God's sacred gift to the world. Through Jesus' life and example we are introduced to God exactly as he is; the God of love, the God of everyone and everything. Jesus' life of service, his self-surrender and death on the cross are not a step away from his true nature. They are not some kind of temporary interruption of his divine existence. Rather, through them we see who God really is.

At communion we remember Jesus – the sacred gift of a gracious God – who invites us to join our small stories to his great story of hope. We re-enact that sacred gift by eating bread and drinking wine together. We celebrate the good news that life is a table, a feast, a banquet, and that we have been invited into Christ's community. We proclaim the story of friendship and reconciliation rather than anger and hostility. We recommit to lay down our own lives for others just as Jesus did for us.

This is why Paul, in his famous letter to the Corinthian Church, which also contains the earliest account of Jesus breaking the bread and passing the wine to his disciples, associates the eucharist or the Lord's supper so strongly with a meal and with the importance of unity.

> In the following directives I have no praise for you, for your meetings do more harm than good. In the first place, I hear that when you come together as a church, there are divisions among you, and to some extent I believe it. No doubt there have to be differences among you to show which of you have God's approval. So then, when you come together, it is not

> the Lord's Supper you eat, for when you are eating, some of you go ahead with your own private suppers. As a result, one person remains hungry and another gets drunk. Don't you have homes to eat and drink in? Or do you despise the church of God by humiliating those who have nothing? What shall I say to you? Shall I praise you? Certainly not in this matter![7]

At the communion table, old factions and grudges should be left behind, and the barriers of hostility, back-biting, envy, competition and rivalry come down. For Paul, the communion table is about our commitment to and solidarity with others, however different they are to us, and about recalling Jesus who loved eating with the outcasts and outsiders and who was a host to everyone.

The ability to give freely, without counting the cost, is a concept we admire and, at the same time, find deeply uncomfortable. We live in a society where the concept that genuine happiness could be derived from serving others appears feeble at least, maybe even contemptible to some. But what if giving, rather than receiving, is the key? What if, in the act of serving – by looking outside of ourselves to the needs of others – we gain more than we could possibly have imagined?

The messages we send to our children tell them that tight-fistedness can't buy them happiness. The greedy are not liberated by their greed, but are imprisoned by it. Those who are selfish misunderstand the purpose of human life. All this is reinforced by a thousand childhood stories and school assemblies. For instance, the cautionary tale of the monkey who puts his hand through the railings to steal some nuts only to discover that his hand is stuck when he tries to pull it back.

In Charles Dickens' perennial classic *A Christmas Carol*, the central character, Ebenezer Scrooge – 'a squeezing, wrenching, grasping, scraping, clutching, covetous, old sinner!'[8] – is redeemed only when he is drawn away from his narrow self-interest and obsession with money. And the ever-popular stories of Robin Hood, Peter Pan, Hansel and Gretel, Cinderella and the *Chronicles of Narnia* by C. S. Lewis all reinforce the same general point: greed leads to misery; generosity to fulfilment.

But here's the odd thing. Whereas all these childhood stories – and many more – contain a clarity of vision which shows avarice, greed and self-centredness in their true ugly colours, in the 'grown-up world' we all get used to the belief that real life somehow works differently.

So it is that we come to learn slowly that our school assemblies were wrong. The truth was to be found in the biology lesson when we were told that life on earth is essentially about the survival of the fittest. It turns out that selfishness – far from being a sin – is actually the universal rule of existence. In the real world, the Scrooges are heroes, the Bob Cratchits are dispensable and the 'Tiny Tims' are unproductive spongers draining the precious resources of the state.[9]

But, forever running counter to all this is the life and example of Jesus, and the outrageous belief that real joy comes through service – as we learn to live by a different story.

22
God in Disguise

'God's appearance changes. Blessed are those who can recognise him in any disguise,' says an old proverb.

It is a sobering fact that the only groups that Jesus ever chose to seriously critique were those who included themselves and yet excluded others from the always-given welcome and embrace of God.

The religious and community leaders of Jesus' day were far from inclusive. Theirs was a culture littered with outcasts. They were accomplished at using their distorted understanding of God to underpin the repressive social hierarchy they had created, which, at one and the same time, put them at the centre of everything and legitimised their exclusion of others.

As far as the Jewish hierarchy were concerned things were clear-cut; people were either acceptable or unacceptable, clean or unclean, in or out, included or excluded. It was black and white – there was no middle ground. The physically disabled, tax collectors, slaves, shepherds, people with leprosy, prostitutes, Romans and all other non-Jews and, to a large degree, all women were considered beyond the pale.

Every day, devout Jews in Jesus' culture would recite thirteen ancient blessings as part of their morning prayer, which included the following:

> *Blessed are You, O Lord our God, King of the Universe, who has not made me a Gentile.*
> *Blessed are You, O Lord our God, King of the Universe, who has not made me a slave.*
> *Blessed are You, O Lord our God, King of the Universe, who has not made me a woman.*[1]

The religious establishment had succeeded in reducing God to nothing more than their own tribal, racist, oppressive and sexist deity. They were God's chosen people; good news for them and those who thought like them, but not for anyone else. What they failed to recognise is that when it turns out that God hates all the same people you do, you can safely conclude that what you've actually done is recreate him in your own image.

Jesus upset the Jewish authorities because he presented a vision of God far bigger than their misconceptions. The God he spoke of was more generous than theirs, more inclusive than theirs, more reckless than theirs – extending mercy to all people regardless, rather than just those deemed good enough, religious enough, healthy enough or orthodox enough to be acceptable.

Jesus not only reminded the hierarchy that their own scriptures taught, 'You shall love your neighbour as yourself';[2] he went on to radically reinterpret and extend the principle even further, as he introduced the revolutionary idea that this approach to relationships should even include their outright adversaries! 'Love your enemies,' he declared. 'Pray for those who persecute you.' In that way you will 'be children of your Father in heaven'.[3]

Which brings us to a rather famous story, told by Jesus in response to the question 'Who is my neighbour?' posed to him one day by one of the nation's religious experts. Jesus replied with what we now call the parable of the Good Samaritan.[4]

A bit of background is needed here: Jews hated Samaritans. They really hated Samaritans. All Samaritans. On any orthodox reading of their scriptures, it was very clear to them that the people of Samaria were persona non grata. In the Israel of Jesus' day, the 'S-word' was a term of contempt and abuse.

Both Jewish and Samaritan religious leaders taught their people that it was absolutely off limits to have any contact with the opposite group. This tension, which sometimes boiled over into outright hostility – between geographical next-door neighbours – went back generations. Samaria had once been part of the old united kingdom of Israel under King David and Solomon his son. But that was before the ten northern tribes of the country proclaimed self-rule, separating from what they perceived to be the rich south and their corrupt royal family.

All this had taken place nearly a millennium before. Since then the northern kingdom had been destroyed by Assyria, and the majority of its people dispersed or taken into captivity, never to return.[5] But the Samaritans had survived and now proudly regarded themselves as the true descendants of those old northern tribes – the guardians of authentic faith in the God of Abraham, Isaac, Jacob and Moses. The leaders of the Jews, however, had a very different take on things. As far as they were concerned, the Samaritans were an apostate group of heretics who practised a corrupt and corrupting faith and who had been rejected by God.[6]

It was in this context that Jesus introduced a very Jewish audience to his story of an abandoned and vulnerable Jew, ignored by two proud members of the Jewish establishment, but eventually helped out by a despised Samaritan traveller. It didn't make easy listening!

Today, you can't help thinking that Jesus might have told a similar story in terms of Protestants and Catholics, Hutus and Tutsis, Sunnis and Shias, Americans and Communists, Jews and Palestinians, or Evangelicals and gays. The point remains the same. The person who acted with generosity, grace and mercy towards someone on the other side of the fence was the one who was a true neighbour.

The sting in the tale is, of course, this. Just as the religious and political leaders of Jesus' day dismissed his views, teaching and behaviour as naïve, morally scandalous and even downright heretical, still today little has changed.

The Quakers have a beautiful saying: 'An enemy is a friend whose story we have not heard.' We are always imprisoned by our exclusion of those who are different from us, never released by it. Besides anything else we need them for our own wholeness, for it is only as we build bridges with those who don't see life our way that we begin to confront and deal with the hidden and ugly parts of our own souls. Without them we are diminished, but through our inclusion and acceptance of them our story becomes richer and deeper than it would have otherwise been – we are stretched and renewed.

In a world where we can be friends with whoever we like, why do we choose only to befriend those who are strikingly similar to us in opinion, outlook, ethnicity and income? In a world where we can believe in any god we like, why do we choose to believe in a protectionist, tribal, exclusive god who is made in our image and confined to the limits of our imagination; a deity who, in the end, is little more than a projection of our own fears and prejudices?

Six months after Nelson Mandela had been inaugurated as president, I had the privilege of visiting the new South Africa. I was working as a presenter for BBC TV and making a programme about the end of the apartheid era and the birth of the 'Rainbow State'. Over one of the most inspiring weeks of my life, I interviewed many of the anti-apartheid movement's key leaders.

I heard first-hand their stories of struggle against the injustice and oppression of the apartheid system. I listened as they told me of the immoral laws that the apartheid government used to entrench and protect their interests over those of the black community. My lasting impression, however, will be that as each of them spoke I recognised the same tone – not just the absence of bitterness towards their former oppressors but the constant gentle sound of forgiveness and of hope for a shared future.

The most challenging and motivating meeting, however, was yet to come. On the last day of my visit I met the elderly Beyers Naudé. A few months later, as this white South African celebrated his eightieth birthday, his friend Nelson Mandela, who always called him 'Oom Bey', would announce to the nation: 'His life is a shining beacon to all South Africans – both black and white. It demonstrates what it means to rise above race, to be a true South African.'

Naudé's father, a minister of the Dutch Reformed Church, was one of the founding members of the *Broederbond* (Brotherhood) – a highly secret, exclusively male, exclusively white, Dutch Reformed society set up to promote Afrikaner supremacy. So powerful was it that every prime minister and president of South Africa from 1948 to the end of the apartheid system in 1994 would be drawn from its ranks.

The young Beyers decided to follow in his father's footsteps by studying theology. He was ordained at twenty-five and also initiated as the youngest ever member of the feared *Broederbond.* For the next twenty years Rev. Beyers Naudé preached with passion his uncompromising message of white superiority and the separation of the races, as 'ordained by God'.

Through what was known as 'Ham theology' the Dutch Reformed Church had developed a system to legitimise their support of apartheid. They taught that the Afrikaners fulfilled a role similar to that of the people of Israel in Old Testament days. The curse placed by Noah on his grandson Canaan (son of Ham) provided a biblical justification for Israel's conquest and enslavement of the Canaanites. Black Africans, or 'Hamites' as they were sometimes called, were also descendants of Canaan.[7]

This teaching was used to justify segregation, and white Afrikaners tightly controlled allocation of living areas for non-whites. The Bible, they said, clearly recognised racial divides – a view based on their reading of the story of the Tower of Babel and a speech given by the apostle Paul at the Areopagus, where he acknowledged that God had 'marked out. . .the boundaries of their lands'.[8]

Naudé explained to me, in a sad but gentle voice, that not only did he use the Bible as a rubber stamp for his racism, but he even attacked as 'anti-Christian' all those who criticised him. 'The scales did not fall from my eyes until the Sharpeville Massacre,' he told me.

On 21 March 1960, a group of around seven thousand black protesters converged on the local police station in the township of Sharpeville, offering themselves up for arrest for not carrying their pass books. The black population of South Africa were always required to carry these books in order to prove, if challenged, that they were not outside their allotted 'homeland' or living area. Failure to produce a pass book on demand would often result in arrest. After a day of demonstrations, the police chose suddenly to open fire. In minutes they had killed sixty-nine people, including numerous children. Many of the victims were shot in the back as they turned to run from the advancing police.

Naudé explained how that day changed him forever. So, one September Sunday morning three years later, tormented by his growing understanding of the real impact of Ham theology, he finally found the courage to preach a sermon in which he condemned apartheid.

The impact was instant. He was forced to resign from his job. He and his family were ostracised by their church and the entire white community. He became an outcast among his own people and the church that he loved. But more was to follow. In 1972 his passport was confiscated and five years later he was placed under permanent house arrest – only allowed to be in the same room with one other person at any time. But the tide of public opinion was slowly turning.

When his 'banning order' was finally lifted in September 1984, Naudé immediately threw himself back into the struggle. The following year he succeeded Desmond Tutu as the Secretary General of the South African Council of Churches and called for the immediate release of all political prisoners, including Nelson Mandela.

Naudé died on 7 September 2004 aged eighty-nine. But by then his vision had become a reality. South Africa had been reborn and Nelson Mandela had served as its first black president. Speaking at his state funeral, Mandela summarised Beyers' life: 'Oom Bey was a brave man,' he said. 'He stood up against apartheid at a time when it was an unpopular thing for whites to do and he did so at the expense of his family and his freedom . . . a true son of Africa.'

In another parable – one about sheep and goats[9] – Jesus tells a story about the end of time to his well-heeled Jewish audience. The King, he says, will gather the nations of the world and then explain to some of those assembled – those who because of their Jewishness are expecting preferential treatment, 'I was hungry and you gave me nothing to eat, I was thirsty and you gave me nothing to drink, I was a stranger and you did not invite me in, I needed clothes and you did not clothe me, I was ill and in prison and you did not look after me.'

Jesus explains that they will answer, 'Lord, when did we see you hungry or thirsty or a stranger or needing clothes or ill or in prison, and did not help you?' But he concludes that the King will reply, 'Truly I tell you, whatever you did not do for one of the least of these, you did not do for me.'

God hides in the oppressed, the poor, the marginalised, the forgotten, the rejected and all those we find challenging. God hides among our neighbours and even our enemies. Our challenge is to look for him in each other's faces; to greet, love and serve all, even when we don't have the sensitivity to recognise God's presence in them at the outset.

Though it appears we never see God, for those with eyes to see, God is to be seen all around us. Though it appears we are able to do nothing in the service of God, for those who look at things with a different lens, there is the constant opportunity to serve God. God is hidden in others all around us.

Jesus' first listeners struggled with the universality of his message. The tragedy is that over the centuries so little has changed. His words still present a giant challenge to the neat and comforting formulas we cling to, which are, as ever, designed to distinguish the clean from the unclean, the acceptable from the unacceptable and the suitable from the unsuitable.

God's appearance changes. Blessed are those who can recognise him in any disguise!

23
Chance Your Arm

The founding father of the ancient people of Israel was Abram, and although the Bible says nothing of his early life, there is an old story which is still taught by Jewish rabbis and Islamic leaders around the world today.[1]

The story explains that Abram's father, Terah, was an idol-maker in the city of Ur in Southern Mesopotamia.[2] However, at an early age, his free-thinking son began to question the authenticity of all these idols. As far as he could see, logically there could only be one God, not many.

As a young man, Abram eventually summoned the courage to confront Terah about all of this. One fateful day, he deliberately broke all his father's idols – except one – before calling his family and wider community to abandon their 'a local god for every occasion' approach to life and to choose instead a new commitment to seek and to worship the one true God; the God of everything and everyone.[3]

But things backfired and, as a reward for this boldness, Abram found himself condemned by Nimrod, the king of Babylon, and thrown into a furnace. Miraculously, however, the fire failed to burn him and he escaped unharmed.[4]

Decades later, as the book of Genesis records,[5] when Abram is an old man, this one God of everything and everyone sets a challenge and makes a promise to him: 'Go from your country, your people and your father's household to the land I will show you. I will make you into a great nation, and I will bless you.'

Right from the start, however, God's intention is clearly that the generosity shown to Abram should be shared universally, so he adds: '. . . and all peoples on earth will be blessed through you.'

I have always loved the statement that follows: 'So Abram went, as the Lord had told him . . .'

Abram – clearly a life-long, pioneering learner – makes the choice to begin the journey of a lifetime with this God of everyone and everything.[6] It is in this context that thirteen years later, when Abram is ninety-nine years of age, God declares that he and his wife Sarai will be blessed with the birth of a son and given new names. Abram becomes Abraham – 'father of multitudes' – and Sarai becomes Sarah – 'princess of the multitude'.[7]

The challenge to Abram and Sarai was to leave the cultural box that had confined them all their lives and to trust the one true God to change their story. Even – perhaps especially – at an elderly age, they had the courage to listen, to venture out and to allow what had become their full stop to give way to the beginning of a whole new challenge and chapter of life. Did this stretch them? Did this scare them? But did it diminish them or set them free?

Nonetheless, still today this journey – the one through which 'all peoples on earth will be blessed' – is not yet complete. And it won't be until we, who also follow the voice of the one God of everyone and everything, learn to make peace with one another, recognising that it is not just us, but all others, even our enemies, who are made in the image of God.

So it is that the same challenge that posed itself to Abram and Sarai back in the Mesopotamian Bronze Age, still confronts each one of us today. Do we have the courage to leave the confines of the boxes that we've lived in – the stories that have dominated our outlook – and choose the adventure of working to bring about a world where every person and every community flourishes, free from oppression, and enjoys living well? Are we ready to work for a world where the excluded are welcomed, the hungry are fed, difference is celebrated, injustice is banished, no one is oppressed and joy is a reality rather than a distant dream?[8]

There was once a man who searched for spiritual reality. He decided that, in order to make himself open to the deepest insights, he should regularly retreat to a cave he knew of in the nearby mountains, for several nights of seclusion and prayer.

He had heard of the great prophets Abraham, Moses and Jesus, and during one retreat, he dared to believe that he had received a miraculous vision about the God they served. He too wanted to live his life as a loyal follower of this same God – the only true God, the God of everyone and everything – rather than the many tribal gods his countrymen believed in.

But as he pondered this possibility, he realised that he faced a huge dilemma. Could he really think about becoming a member of the official religion of the old Roman Empire that had constantly threatened the security, culture and very existence of his people, and that did so in Christ's name? Would accepting the Christian faith amount to becoming a traitor to his country? And how could he expect his fellow countrymen to embrace a faith that was wrapped up in the conquest-driven militarism of the world's most dangerous power bloc, and driven by values that stood in such stark contradiction to those of Christ himself?

At the same time, however, he believed that the one true God had spoken to all humanity through these great men and that their teaching and example should be followed. More than that, he also felt that the God of everyone and everything was leading him to bring this wonderful revelation, not only to the people of his country but, of course, to the whole world. So, what should he do? What were his options?

He couldn't become Jewish, since the Jewish people didn't accept Jesus as a legitimate prophet of the one true God. But nor could he affiliate to the faith of the empire. There was only one other option: to articulate his vision of a worldwide, monotheistic faith beyond the confines of either Judaism or imperial Christianity.

The man's name was Muhammad.[9]

It is all about those cultural spectacles. Never underestimate the power of the story you live in to shape you.

One way of interpreting and telling the story of Muslim history is to say that Muhammad, a false prophet, received a demonic vision and that, turning his back on, or being ignorant of, the teachings of the Church, he created a counterfeit religion that holds countless millions of people in darkness. It's a version of the story that I was told a thousand times – and, of course, there are Muslim equivalents about the Jesus story. But it is a version of the story that can only ever create division, enmity, distrust and conflict – it is quite literally a dead end!

My Muslim friends have a phrase 'Allahu akbar', which they tell me means not only that 'God is great' but that 'God is greatest'; greater than our understanding, greater than any of our ideas about God. I think they are right and that this is what Jesus came to demonstrate. God belongs to no one, and to everyone. God is not a tribal deity but the Creator of the whole earth and all people.

Abraham Lincoln once replied to an enquirer who was keen to know whether God was on the side of those who sought the emancipation of America's slaves: 'Sir, my concern is not whether God is on our side; my greatest concern is to be on

God's side, for God is always right.'[10] Naturally, if we have spent our whole lives imagining God to be on 'our side' it is disturbing, disorientating, challenging and even frightening to entertain the idea that God belongs to others as well as us.

For all those who follow Jesus, however, none of this should come as a shock; after all, two-thirds of our Bible – the entire Old Testament – is really the Hebrew scriptures, where it is assumed that God is a Jew. And Jesus himself remained a Jew all his life, showing no obvious inclination to create a non-Jewish religion. Christianity is, in fact, of its very nature a multi-faith tradition, a synergy of large aspects of Judaism along with 'baptised' ideas from other ancient religious cultures blended together around the figure of Jesus Christ and what he uniquely brings to the world.[11]

I continue to be captivated by the person of Jesus. There are many other remarkable human beings in the history of the world's religions, some of whom I admire massively; but for me, Jesus is the complete revelation of God. If it looks like Jesus, it is God. He is the one I have chosen to follow and around whom the work of Oasis has been built over the decades. But it is because of this allegiance, not in spite of it, that I respect the faith of others. More than this, as I interact with people of other backgrounds, cultures and religions I constantly find myself both challenged and inspired by them as well as deepened in my sense of the uniqueness of the message of Jesus. Ignorance, I have learnt, is never bliss – however hard you try to dress it up. Burying our heads in the sand never makes us stronger, or wiser, but simply leaves us blind and vulnerable.

It is an extraordinarily dogmatic stance to imagine that somehow the group or community that we happen to belong to has, by an astonishing stroke of fortune, ended up with a monopoly on truth – the whole truth and nothing but the truth, with no remainder! Unfortunately, it is also depressingly common, as is the conclusion that, as a result, there is no need of dialogue with, or benefit from, other cultures, worldviews and faiths that surround us.

The essence of genuine discussion is that each person in that discussion is open to the possibility of being changed by what is shared. Without this, we might as well stand in front of a mirror and talk to ourselves. The great Catholic missionary and theologian Vincent Donovan put it like this: 'Do not try to call [others] to where you are, as beautiful as that place may seem to you. You must have the courage to go with them to a place neither you nor they have been before.'[12]

Humanity has to reach the position where, at the same time as being committed to our own beliefs and traditions – indeed, because of being committed to our own beliefs and traditions – we can live peacefully and constructively with members of other faiths.[13] It is essential that we prioritise dialogue and common activity instead of letting tensions between faiths and cultures threaten the stability of societies and even global peace.

I have learnt that genuine friendships are the irreplaceable cornerstone of the kind of productive conversations that will enable us to navigate a path to peace, even when confronted by the most challenging issues. And this principle is universal; it applies as much to community and international relationships as it does to personal and family ones.

The tragedy is that across the millennia religion has, all too often, been at the heart of war and bloodshed. The strength of faith in the twenty-first century must lie in a moral voice that, rather than attempting to coerce through dogma, will appeal to and embrace all people through humility and the genuine recognition that everyone is created in the image of the God of everyone and everything.

None of this is to suggest that we are looking for some bland kind of blended soup of a society where all our distinctives and differences have been dissolved and we settle for the lowest common denominator. Rather, our goal must be a vigorous and healthy society where, through open dialogue and mutual commitment to each other, we can learn, grow and change, and so achieve a strong and robust peace, yet still maintain the integrity of our own faith.

Just before he was murdered, Martin Luther King Jr wrote:

> We have inherited a large house, a great 'world house' in which we have to live together – black and white, Easterner and Westerner, Gentile and Jew, Catholic and Protestant, Moslem and Hindu – a family unduly separated in ideas,

cultures, and interest, who, because we can never again live apart, we must somehow learn to live with each other in peace.

We must learn to live together as brothers or perish together as fools.

The future safety of our world hinges around '*world-house*' people who will embrace diversity, upholding their own faith and culture while affirming the faith and culture of others. People who will work together for a global culture of justice, real friendship and compassion. It's this type of persistence that runs through the centre of God's love for us, and must find an echo in us and our work. The world is crying out for us to work together to find a better way of being human, and the best way of achieving this is to pursue it in grass-roots situations.

In St Patrick's Cathedral, Dublin, stands what is known as the 'Door of Reconciliation'. Back in 1492 this door was all that separated two feuding Irish families as the Butlers of Ormond sought sanctuary from the Fitzgeralds of Kildare. Realising that the fighting had been getting out of control, Gerald Fitzgerald pleaded with 'Black James' Butler to accept a truce and open the door. But, suspecting treachery, Black James refused. In response Gerald proceeded to hack a hole in it and 'chance his arm' by thrusting it through as a pledge of his goodwill. This daring gesture proved enough. The door was opened and peace was achieved.

Go ahead. Chance your arm!

24

Upside Down and Inside Out

Chance your arm.
Live generously.
Act courageously.
Love wildly, even the people that hate you.
Pray for the people that hate you.
Don't be a slave to the rule book.
Copy God, the great law breaker.

This seems a fairly faithful summary of Jesus' words. Read the following to see whether you agree:

> You have heard that it was said, 'Eye for eye, and tooth for tooth.' But I tell you, do not resist an evil person. If anyone slaps you on the right cheek, turn to them the other cheek also. And if anyone wants to sue you and take your shirt, hand over your coat as well. If anyone forces you to go one mile, go with them two miles. Give to the one who asks you, and do not turn away from the one who wants to borrow from you.

> You have heard that it was said, 'Love your neighbour and hate your enemy.' But I tell you, love your enemies and pray for those who persecute you, that you may be children of your Father in heaven. He causes his sun to rise on the evil and the good, and sends rain on the righteous and the unrighteous. If you love those who love you, what reward will you get? Are not even the tax collectors doing that? And if you greet only your own people, what are you doing more than others? Do not even pagans do that? Be perfect, therefore, as your heavenly Father is perfect.[1]

But here's the question. Would it not be extraordinarily inconsistent, indeed downright hypocritical, for God to encourage us to love our enemies and seek the best for our detractors and persecutors, if, without recompense, he is not able to do the same?

The cross on which Jesus was executed 2,000 years ago, just outside the city of Jerusalem, has become the universal symbol – the single most important visual identifier – of the Christian faith. It is ubiquitous. It decorates everything from churches and cathedrals, earrings and necklaces, to denim jackets and graveyards.[2] But, for all its popularity, there is still a huge amount of confusion around exactly what it was all about.

It has often been suggested that the crucifixion of Christ was the outcome of God's anger with the sin and failure of humanity; in other words, all that is wrong with us! God's wrath over our behaviour could only be appeased through a punishment that fits the crime. And the crime deserved the death penalty. God demanded justice. Someone had to pay. But, because of his 'love' for us, he chose to orchestrate the violent death of his innocent Son in our guilty place. Hence, we are forgiven.

One of the many moral problems with all this (and there are lots of them) is, of course, that, if it is true, Jesus' teaching is instantly reduced to a case of 'do as God says, not as God does'. On the one hand, God is, Jesus taught, the God of grace and goodness, but, on the other, one of the central acts of the Christian faith is bound up with God's simmering anger and relentless quest for retribution. If violence, hostility and the need for 'pay-back' characterise God's identity, how on earth can we aspire to be like him by being non-violent, non-hostile and non-vengeful?

The error in this kind of thinking is unmasked by what is perhaps the most profound theological statement in the whole of the Bible: 'God is love'.[3] If this is true, love is more than a quality that God possesses; it is his very essence. Rather than love being a virtue that characterises God's attitude on a good day, it is instead his essential and unchangeable nature.

Those who have swallowed the line about God's wrath will, of course, respond that surely, if God is love, he must also experience anger at injustice. Of course. But even we know that by its very nature love always involves risk on the part of the lover and never comes with the guarantee that it will be reciprocated rather than rejected.

Some years ago I had the opportunity to ask a rabbi, one of the UK's senior Jewish leaders, about the concept of God's anger. I will never forget his answer. 'It is perhaps better, and far more accurate,' he said, 'to understand God's anger as his anguish – a dimension of his love, but never an emotion in opposition to it.'

Every parent understands the sense, as well as the challenge, of that statement. All of us who know the joy of having children also know, to a greater or lesser extent, the disappointment, heartache and anguish sometimes caused by their attitudes, behaviour or even downright rebelliousness. Yet no balanced or caring parent has ever sought retribution. And every parent has learnt that whenever our anger gets the better of us and operates outside the context of our love, it leaves us filled with regret and having to say sorry.

The cross is not about God's anger, cruelty, violence and longing for retribution. Instead, it's the opposite. It is about humanity's anger, cruelty, violence and longing for retribution. And it's about God's dogged love.[4] On the cross, Jesus does not placate God's anger as he takes the punishment for sin, but rather he absorbs the consequences of all the injustice and sin around him. 'The world breaks everyone,' wrote Ernest Hemingway. 'But those that will not break it kills. It kills the very good and the very gentle and the very brave impartially.'[5]

History records that Jesus died because of the self-interest of the Jewish leaders, the pride of the Roman Empire, the detachment and weakness of Pontius Pilate (the Roman official in charge of Judea at the time), the manipulation of Judas and the fickleness of the ordinary people.

'Jesus shouldered the burden, not so much of "sin" in the abstract,' writes N. T. Wright,

> in a kind of transaction which took place away from the actual events that led to his death, but rather of the actual weight – the power and results – of human sin and rebellion, the accumulation of the actual human pride, sin, folly and shame which, at that moment in history, concentrated themselves in the arrogance of Rome, the self-seeking of the Jewish leaders, and the distorted dreams of the Jewish revolutionaries, and the failures of Jesus' own followers.[6]

Besides anything else, the cross demonstrates that Jesus practises what he preaches. He has the courage to take his own medicine. He goes the extra mile. He lays down his life. He refuses to return evil for evil. Instead, he willingly absorbs its impact within his own body.

To recall Gandhi's comment to Charlie Andrews, Jesus takes a blow, several blows, and shows that though he will not strike back, nor will he be turned aside. He demonstrates that the only pathway to peace is the way of peace itself.

Just as a lightning conductor soaks up powerful and destructive bolts of electricity, so Jesus, as he hung on the cross, soaked up – but refused to return – the hate, rejection, pain and alienation all around him. And, in doing so, he was demonstrating to his contemporaries what a true Messiah or liberator looks like. Real freedom is not delivered through aggression, it cannot be maintained by force and it is never enjoyed by those who are driven by their anger. Just like peace, it only ever takes root, is nurtured and reaches maturity, in the soil of self-giving love.

That extraordinary cry of Jesus, as he hung dying on the cross – 'My God, my God, why have you forsaken me?' – helps us get right to the heart of what was happening on that hillside outside the city of Jerusalem.[7]

I once spoke on an away weekend for a church youth group. Without doubt the award, over those few days, for the wittiest and most endearing character present would have gone to Jason. He was the life and soul of the whole party; a sixteen-year-old, all-round great kid who was loved by everyone. But tragically, seven days later, Jason lay dead; killed instantly when the moped he was riding was in collision with a double-decker bus.

Several weeks after the funeral had taken place, a friend of Jason's family phoned me. His parents had asked whether I would visit them. I will never forget the conversation we had together. We sat in almost complete silence for some time before they spoke. But when they did, they couldn't stop. It was as though all the pressure of the last couple of months was suddenly released and their raw emotion poured out into the room.

Why had God let them down? Why had he stolen their son? Why had he robbed Jason of the gift of life, or, at least, watched unconcerned and inactive while the paramedics fought to resuscitate his motionless body in the road? What had they done wrong? Why was he punishing them? Why didn't he answer their prayers? Why was God so distant and silent when they needed him most? They felt so abandoned, so forgotten and so ignored.

As the pain of Jason's mother and father's searing questions drilled themselves into my soul, I suddenly realised that they were utterly reminiscent of Jesus' cry of anguish from his cross, 'My God, my God, why have you deserted me?'

As a child I had been taught that God deliberately turned his back on Jesus as he hung on the cross. God, I was told, did this because the sight of Jesus, as he took onto himself the punishment for the world's mess and failure, was an affront to God's moral purity. Indeed, as a young adult, knowing no better, I had often passed on that same understanding to others. But now, watching Jason's mum and dad, I suddenly saw how wrong-headed, misguided, disempowering and guilt-inducing all this was.

It happens that Jesus' cry of abandonment from the cross is a direct quote from the lyrics of Psalm 22; one of the most ruthlessly honest songs ever written by King David. More than this, the emotion behind it has been echoed constantly, not just by Jason's mum and dad, but by countless millions of people through the centuries, as they have suffered bereavement, depression, redundancy, enslavement, divorce, rejection, oppression, disease, abuse, poverty, starvation and violence – 'If God is really love, then where is he? Why has he deserted me?'

As he suffered, Jesus experienced exactly what so many of us are overcome by in life's darkest and hardest moments: the feeling of being alone, abandoned by God; of perhaps even doubting God's very existence. The uncompromising honesty of Jesus' cry on the cross mirrors those of countless millions of people who suffer pain or oppression. It shouts not of the differentness of his situation from ours but rather of his identification and solidarity with us.

But here comes the twist! For those who linger long enough to look more deeply at Psalm 22, they soon discover that this is a poem which, through its raw emotion, reaches an unexpected conclusion. Though, in the agony of his physical and spiritual pain, Jesus never gets further than the first line, this psalm, as he knew very well, eventually speaks triumphantly of God: 'I will declare [his] name to my people . . . for he has not despised or scorned the suffering of the afflicted one; he has not hidden his face from him but has listened to his cry for help.'[8]

Psalm 22, just like the whole Bible, is the narrative of a loving God's unerring refusal to separate himself from us. It is this always present sense of hope, drawn from the fact that God is not absent in our struggles, that Jesus clings to as he echoes those ancient words originally penned by King David.

From the cross, as Jesus opens his mouth and howls his devastating cry, death seems stronger than love. Through Jesus' tears, the God of love seems to be conspicuous only by his absence. When we are caught in the teeth of suffering, our prayers often feel so futile. Our fight, it seems, is not just against the odds, but against the silence, or indifference, of God himself. But even in his darkest and most disturbed moment, Christ reminds himself that beyond the horizon of his feelings and emotions lies a greater truth.

As I listened to Jason's mother and father, I realised that the Bible never patronises us with the trite promise that, if we believe, life will hold no misery, heartache, despair or questions. Following Christ does not come with a 'get out of jail' escape from pain, complexity and doubt – nor does it ensure a constant sense of God's closeness.

Jesus' unflinching cry for help shows us that in those moments when we too ask questions of God and wait for apparently non-existent responses, we are not alone. While the depth of our struggle or suffering may cause us to believe that God has abandoned us, the reality, if we trust Christ's experience, is that he is always right there with us, in the suffering.

The cross of Jesus stands at the centre of our pain-ridden world – thrust into the dirt to proclaim not 'God is absent' but 'God is here!'

In 2007, an astonishing book was published. *Come Be My Light* is a collection of forty, never-before-made-available, private letters written by Mother Teresa to her closest friends over a period of sixty-six years![9]

The letters, which her colleagues had wanted to be destroyed but which the Vatican ordered to be preserved, reveal that for vast parts of her life Teresa felt no presence of God whatsoever. Although perpetually cheery in public, she often lived in a state of deep spiritual pain. She bemoans her 'darkness', 'loneliness', 'dryness' and 'torture', and speaks of living 'in the tunnel'.

In 1948, shortly after beginning her work in the slums of Calcutta with the poor, sick and dying, Teresa wrote, 'Where is my faith? Even deep down there is nothing but emptiness and darkness.' In 1953 she wrote, 'Please pray specially for me that I may not spoil his work and that our Lord may show himself – for there is such terrible darkness within me, as if everything was dead. It has been like this more or less from the time I started the work.'

Years later Teresa confided, 'I am told God lives in me – and yet the reality of darkness and coldness and emptiness is so great that nothing touches my soul . . . I want God with all the power of my soul – and yet between us there is terrible separation.' In another letter she confessed: 'I feel just that terrible pain of loss, of God not wanting me, of God not being God, of God not really existing.' And although she found a way to accept this frequent sense of God's absence, she never overcame it. In a 1995 letter she discussed her continuing 'spiritual dryness'. She died, two years later, in 1997, aged eighty-seven.

When I read Mother Teresa's words I found them a liberation – an echo of Jesus' cry from the cross, 'My God, my God, why have you forsaken me?' and a comfort in my own experience of life.

When it comes to belief in God, our world is full of doubters – all the way from archbishops to atheists. We all live with uncertainty. Ironically, however, those who choose the pathway of faith are, by virtue of that very choice, likely to encounter deeper and more challenging dilemmas than those who never begin the journey.

In truth, doubt isn't the opposite of faith; it walks hand in hand with it. Faith and doubt are inextricably linked. Without room for doubt, faith could not exist. Instead, the only remaining option would be blind acceptance of incontrovertible fact.[10] Real faith has no easy answers. Life has taught me that it is far better to belong to a community that has the courage to articulate and debate hard questions without necessarily settling them, than to one that tries to ignore and bury those questions without even asking them.

Teresa's courage allowed her to embrace her vulnerability rather than attempt to disguise and deny it. Many of us find this level of openness difficult because we perceive vulnerability as weakness. We want to be in control – which of course is why we like certainty and rules. To be seen as vulnerable scares us. But life is imperfect. It is filled with struggle. To be alive is therefore to be vulnerable, which means that when we try to avoid our vulnerability, we deny ourselves the fulfilment of living wholeheartedly.

What marked Mother Teresa apart was not the depth of her doubts and questions about life and God, but her strength and honesty in asking those questions of God. Rather than representing a failure of faith, the agonising of Teresa's writings demonstrates a deep faith in God's reality which she refused to abandon, even in the face of his seeming silence and her sense of emotional disconnection from him. Real faith knows doubt well, and sometimes chooses to live in conscious defiance of it.

But though the cross is part of the story, it is not the whole story!

The cross without the resurrection is a bitter blow. Its message, in the end, is nothing more than violence wins, might is right, and the weak will always be oppressed, downtrodden and abused by the powerful. Privilege, position, money and the gun rule. Without the resurrection the cross is an impotent symbol of failure and defeat. Without the resurrection Jesus is just another victim of the ultimate method of exclusion: death itself.

But three short days after they had torn Jesus' limp carcass down from the gibbet, where they had skewered and taunted him as he hung dying, he had slipped right through their grasp. Apathy, envy, jealousy, hatred, pride, anger, lies, cowardliness, gossip and duplicity had all conspired together to crush him. They had done their worst – but this was his answer. The resurrection turns the tables – it transforms everything. Love is stronger than death, service more powerful than manipulation.

Through his life, death and resurrection, Jesus takes on the forces of darkness, intolerance, self-interest and evil on their own terms, and wins. In doing so, however, he will not use the tools of evil itself – those of coercion, force, domination and violence. Instead, through weakness, he confounds the powerful. Slowly, he lures the wielders of unjust power into exposing and discrediting themselves. Jesus, creatively and courageously, armed only with the non-violent power of truth and love, opposes and defeats injustice. He soaks up all that can be thrown at him. He contains evil, but evil cannot contain him.

Christ's resurrection destroys the misconception that power and aggression win. You can crucify love, and bury it behind a huge stone, but you can't keep it there! Death has no power over love. Love creates something new even out of the destruction caused by death; it bears everything and overcomes everything. What is more, it does its most revolutionary work where the power of death is strongest, in war and persecution and homelessness and hunger and even in the face of physical death itself.

The resurrection is the declaration that Jesus is right; that the peace-makers are really blessed. You can put his philosophy for life up against any other on offer because it works. You can trust him with your life. More than that, it is short-sighted to live any other way, because to do so is to be out of step with the way that the world actually is; the way that God is – the upside-down principle of power through vulnerability and love.

Jesus spoke of losing one's life in order to gain it, as opposed to clinging to it and so losing it. 'If you want to become my followers,' he said, 'deny yourself, take up your cross, and follow me.'[11] In this way he invites all those who choose to follow him to enter an upside-down world, an inside-out world; a world where all the things people normally assume about human flourishing are set aside and a new order is established.

Those who are determined to walk the way of Christ may well be laughed at by others for 'taking it all too far', for getting things out of proportion, for being fanatical, idealistic or naïve. They may even face persecution and rejection. But they are on their way to becoming the human being they were meant to be.

Pick up your cross and follow Jesus!

Live a different kind of story!

25

Better Together

Over the last few months we've worked on a new invitation to Oasis Church in Waterloo. It reads like this:

> Welcome to Oasis Church Waterloo.
> Here we try to practise the generous gospel of Jesus Christ.
> This means you will be mixing with:
> Seekers, searchers and those who have been bruised,
> those who rejoice and those who mourn,
> those who are worn out, burnt out and exhausted,
> those for whom life is filled with purpose and direction,
> those in fulfilling relationships and those who have failed to love, been cheated in love or who are afraid to receive love,
> those of various nationalities and sexualities,
> those who are strong in their faith and those who are besieged by questions and doubts,
> those rejected by other churches and those who have found meaningful community here for the first time,
> those who have broken their promises,
> those who have been betrayed,

those bowed down with burdens,
those for whom the grip of alcohol or work, drugs or sex, money or unnamed powers is getting stronger and those for whom that grip is loosening,
and goodness knows how many others . . .
indeed anyone like those Jesus chose to spend his time with.

This is not a private club – it is a community open to all people of goodwill.

And, though we are not yet strong and vulnerable enough to show the unconditional love of God at all times,
we hope we are moving in that direction.

Welcome to Oasis Church Waterloo.[1]

Superman, Wonder Woman, The Green Lantern, Thor, Captain America, Spiderman, Black Widow, Wolverine . . . we love a superhero. Then there's that even rarer character, the costumed crime fighter who, underneath the uniform, is made of exactly the same stuff as you and me. Take Batman, the masked vigilante who, without a single superpower to his name, and armed only with a cape, a strong sense of duty and a clear moral code (plus some pretty impressive technology!), dedicated his life to fearlessly protecting the good citizens of Gotham City, without any expectation of reward or recognition.[2]

This idea, however – the notion of the isolated heroic individual, who is always calm and always in control; who shows no fear; who weighs, judges, decides and acts decisively and independently with no need for support of any kind from the wider community – plays a much larger role in shaping our lives than simply in relation to what we choose to watch, or not, on the big screen.[3]

'It is a bizarre development in the tide of history', writes Mike Riddell, 'that we have become so isolated from one another that we have begun to regard our self-contained separation with a certain amount of pride. Those who can function without significant support from others are described as independent and self-reliant, while our desire for relationship is treated as evidence of some weakness.'[4]

Never in human history has it been easier – indeed, almost compulsory – to do your own thing. Our belief that everyone should be free to discover themselves and their own values is enshrined in the popular mantra we all learn by heart: 'I'll do it my way.' Indeed, the unsaid but common assumption of our culture is that society itself exists primarily to assist the development of the individual and the fulfilment of their needs, desires and goals.

The truth, however, is very different. We are impoverished by our isolation. Though we spend so much of our time pursuing our own agendas and fulfilment, at exactly the same time the unending quest of every human being is to shatter their loneliness that, as Mother Teresa once observed, is one of the most prevalent and depressing diseases of the Western world. As the saying goes: 'A man wrapped up in himself makes a very small bundle.'[5]

The philosopher René Descartes famously commented: 'I think, therefore I am', but we all somehow sense that a far more honest assessment of life is found in the African proverb: 'I am because you are; you are because we are. Every person is a person through other people.' All of which brings us right back to that statement from the first page of the Bible – and an extraordinary example of how a society can read one thing, yet see another:

> *So God created mankind in his own image,*
> *in the image of God he created them;*
> *male and female he created them.*[6]

The message is very clear: it is as humanity together that we are made in God's image. Life is about 'we' not 'me'. The kind of individualism that has become such a key feature of our Western world is utterly foreign to the writer of these words in Genesis. Rather than conceiving of people in the overly individualistic terms that we are familiar with today, on its very first page the Bible recognises that we are not 'independent' but 'interdependent'; all inherently connected to the rest of the human community.

Human beings are social beings. We can never become our true selves in isolation. We are most human when we are connected to others and are always diminished and de-humanised by our disconnection from one another. Belonging alone gives purpose and meaning to life, because we are designed not only with the capacity for, but also with the deep need of, community.

One of the biggest weaknesses in our society is the lack of self-knowing. How many people do you know whose greatest weakness in life is that they are unaccountable? Nobody ever tells them what they really need to know about themselves – what everybody else already knows about them and often talks about together behind their backs!

It is impossible to become the person you were meant to be outside the context of a community. Not only do we learn directly from the example of others, but our interaction with them hones and corrects our responses. The Bible urges us to 'spur one another on towards love and good deeds'.[7]

It is only together that ordinary people like us are set free to achieve the extraordinary. As isolated individuals we simply lack the moral and ethical resources we need to become the people we were meant to be. We need the help of one another as we seek to identify and develop the moral habits and skills that will enable us to become the kind of people we want to be. Equally, we need the help of one another as we seek to recognise and overcome the faults and flaws that hold us back from becoming the kind of people we want to be. This, of course, means that instead of spending time worrying about how to maintain our independence, the real question we should be asking and answering is: 'What sort of community, with what sort of story, do I need to be a part of in order to become the person I was meant to be?'

Learning to be moral is, as we've discovered, just like learning any other skill. We learn good habits by watching people with good habits, as well as practising them ourselves. A person becomes generous by imitating generous people; compassionate by imitating compassionate people. We become just or merciful, faithful, self-controlled or caring by imitating others; others from the community whose teaching, example and story model a character and lifestyle worth imitating.

All this means that mentoring is just as essential to the task of moral and spiritual formation as it is to musical and mathematical development. If learning to love our enemies is an idea or theory, it is both harder to imagine and extremely easy to dismiss. But when I see someone I respect act it out, or when I learn by trying it out myself, not only is it harder to dismiss, but slowly the principles become embedded.

There is nothing as helpful as a morally and spiritually inexperienced person having the opportunity to look over the shoulder of, and be coached by, a morally mature and spiritually wise person. And as through life we develop these skills and disciplines, in time we too will be called upon to play our role in mentoring others, both formally and informally.[8] There is just no substitute for examples of Christ-centred living wrapped up in human form.

This is why the strongest communities are multi-generational. A community comprised solely of twenty- and thirty-somethings will be impoverished and will run the risk of producing spiritual and ethical pygmies. A community comprised simply of fifty- and sixty-somethings will suffer the danger of their wisdom turning sour, and of their energy – for the challenge and opportunity of life – drying up. The task of every healthy community is the creation of people who are better than they would have been without the support of one another.

We can only thrive in communities where we are known, accepted, loved, nurtured and held accountable, and where honest confrontation is valued, even though we know the process may sometimes be painful at first. This requires of me both accountability and humility: the accountability to others that enables them to offer me honest feedback and guidance, and the humility that enables me both to recognise my weaknesses and to be open to their input.

There are, of course, countless day-to-day challenges to living all this out, but inclusivity was never a matter of 'anything goes', of sweeping awkward issues under the carpet, of turning a blind eye, ducking confrontation and hoping for the best. Although inclusion never demands conformity, and agreement is not a condition of acceptance, neither is it about excusing one individual to the detriment of others.[9]

I've slowly learnt that any community that seeks peace has to have the courage to confront the situations that are preventing it, rather than just avoiding them. Real peace is only possible in a community that is strong enough not to shy away from such a challenge. Jesus famously remarked that 'The truth will set you free.' What he didn't promise was that it wouldn't hurt along the way sometimes.[10]

Hounded by a nagging sense of vulnerability and a lack of self-worth, we learn to affirm ourselves over-against one another – and often over-against God. Real freedom is born, however, not from insistence on our independence, but from getting connected. Only this gives us a true perspective. Hard as it may be, and contrary to all our culture tells us, the first step to freedom is that of abandoning our autonomy. It takes many of us far too long to learn that although it is tough to belong – to be committed to the hard work of being part of a community – there is only one other option, and that is even harder: not to belong to and be committed to a community!

Besides being a writer, John Donne was Dean of St Paul's Cathedral in London. It was just before his death in 1631 that he penned his famous words:

> All mankind is of one author, and is one volume . . . No man is an island, entire of itself; every man is a piece of the continent, a part of the main . . . any man's death diminishes me, because I am involved in mankind; and therefore never send to know for whom the bell tolls; it tolls for thee.[11]

A culture of 'heroic individualism' is the stuff of mythology, rather than everyday reality. The only way to thrive – to become the people we were meant to be – is to break free of the tyranny of the detachment and individualism in which our society is soaked. We are made from the materials of our communal life, so whenever we cut back these attachments and commitments, we shrink rather than grow.

The mystery of the universe is such that our very formation as a human being requires the participation of others. No life even comes into being in isolation. Each one of us is the product of community. The legacy of our genes is a demonstration of the fact that we are essentially dependent beings. Our lives are inseparably bound up with others from their very beginning.

Jesus' understanding of life was soaked in these ideas. In ancient Hebrew thought, real knowledge and wisdom were never to be found alone in a library or in abstract, theoretical ideas, but rather could only be experienced, embraced and discovered through relationship, experience and interdependence.[12]

In the Oscar-winning film *Good Will Hunting*, therapist Sean Maguire (played by Robin Williams) forms a relationship with Will Hunting, a young man who is a troubled genius on the wrong side of the law (played by Matt Damon), and tries to help him with his gift and his life. Sat together on a park bench, Maguire explains that there is a difference, for instance, between knowing facts about art from books, and experiencing the awe of gazing at the ceiling of the Sistine chapel; and between appreciating poetry about warfare, and being caught in the chaos and carnage of a battlefield yourself. He talks to Hunting about finding the courage to live life instead of retreating and using his intellect as an escape mechanism.

> 'I'd ask you about love, you'd probably quote me a sonnet. But you've never looked at a woman and been totally vulnerable . . .

'You don't know about real loss, 'cause it only occurs when you've loved something more than you love yourself. And I doubt you've ever dared to love anybody that much.

'You're an orphan, right? Do you think I'd know the first thing about how hard your life has been, how you feel, who you are, 'cause I read *Oliver Twist*? Does that encapsulate you?'[13]

The Hebrew word that sums all this up is *yada*, and perhaps the best definition of this extraordinary little term that I've ever come across is 'to know completely and to be completely known'. *Yada* cannot be gained by standing back from life. It requires active, ongoing, hands-on, life-to-life, intentional engagement. It is about far more than information, much more than theory. It demands relationship and experience – it can only be learnt through trial and error, love and laughter, success and disappointment, service and sacrifice, joy and pain.[14]

Understanding this means that it should come as no surprise that the Hebrew language contains no separate word for the concept of 'spirituality'. Instead, what we now refer to as 'spiritual' was understood simply as a constituent part of a life that was complete, integrated and whole; and the word for that was *shalom*.[15]

This integrated view is the bedrock of the way that Jesus thought and taught about life. For him there was no distinction between the physical, material world and some kind of separate or detached 'spiritual' world; instead, they were joined up.[16]

Human beings are neither physical bodies with a spiritual side, nor spiritual beings somehow trapped in physical bodies; instead, we represent the full integration of the physical with the spiritual. So when people say things like, 'I'm a spiritual person', they're on to a deep truth, whereas when others protest, 'I'm not spiritual', the most honest response is: 'It's too late; you're human!'[17]

We are designed for relationship; with other people and with God. This is what Jesus meant when he taught that he had come to offer 'life to the full'.[18]

In our twenty-first-century 'dis-integrated' Western culture, life has become compartmentalised and spirituality is generally regarded as something 'a little aside' from the rest of life. As a result, a human being can end up very far from being human. The problem is that although we know that true well-being is dependent on the full integration of life – physically, morally, socially and spiritually – we struggle to be able to talk about it. We just don't have the 'joined-up' vocabulary available in the English language to allow us to do it, which means that we are painfully inarticulate when it comes to our ability to express or explore our moral and spiritual development.

Somehow, because of this, even in the very process of affirming and valuing spirituality, we too often end up turning our backs on the greater truth: that all of life is a spiritual experience, and therefore each moment is part of our spiritual development. Our thoughts, feelings, friendships, skills, learning styles, creativity, imagination, work, family – all these things are very human and, at one and the same time, spiritual. Indeed, in Jesus' thought, these elements of life were no less 'spiritual' than the prayer or liturgy of the priest or religious leader.[19] Instead, the whole of life was an integrated package.

The entire universe is one vast sacred space. Everything has the possibility to mediate the divine. We should look for the spiritual in every human interaction and relationship; and learn to celebrate Christ's presence in every moment, every meal, every smile and every conversation, because it is together that we slowly become the human beings that we were always meant to be!

The old man was crippled and in a wheelchair. Since the untimely death of his wife many years before he had lived alone.

One day he was invited to the wedding of a young girl who lived on his street. He threw the invitation in the bin but, at the last moment, something strange came over him and he decided to go.

At the reception he talked to the bride and the groom. They asked him about his own wedding day. He told them about the music that had been played and the dancing that had been done.

As he spoke, he began to hum one of the old tunes. He got louder and louder, and his foot began to tap to the music.

Slowly others joined in, and, in time, he burst into song.

Then, before he knew what he was doing, he was out of

the wheelchair and dancing before all the guests, to show them how the steps had gone.

Everyone marvelled to see the crippled man dancing.

And, all those years leading up to that day, he thought that he had forgotten the tune.[20]

A Last Word

The King

There once lived a king who was so unpleasant, angry and mean that it showed on his face. Everyone in his kingdom feared and hated him. When he rode out among his people, with his face contorted in mean ugliness, they would scatter and run away. If caught off guard they would bow low and avert their eyes in silence, their dislike and fear of him showing on their faces. In return, the king would mumble, mutter and sputter mean things to them as he rode by.

Slowly, the king grew even angrier with his subjects because of how they treated him. But the angrier he got, the more they despised him. Finally, out of frustration, he called for his wisest wizard and said, 'I am tired of how the people treat me. Use your magic to make them nicer people. I command it.'

The wizard thought long and hard about this order. It was a tough one. Finally, he explained that in order to make his subjects nicer people, the king would have to do exactly what he told him to do. The king agreed. 'Good,' he said. 'Whatever you ask, I will do. Anything that is necessary to get those rotten, ungrateful people to treat me the way I deserve.' He grumbled a bit more under his breath and settled his face into its ugliest, meanest grimace.

The wizard went into a high cabinet and took down a box, which he carefully opened. Inside was a mask of the king's own face. It bore such a life-like resemblance to him that the king's mouth fell wide open when he saw it. But there was one small difference. The expression on the mask was smiling – almost radiant – instead of being mean, angry and menacing. 'Where did you get such a mask?' enquired the king. 'Never mind,' said the wizard. 'The point is that it's a magic mask. Here is what you must do, as you agreed, to the letter. You must put this mask on now and not, under any circumstances, take it off for 100 days. It will make the people love you.'

'What . . . why . . . I . . . I am not wearing that! They will lose respect for me. I can't do it. I won't do it!'

'It's your choice,' said the wizard, 'but you agreed and this is the best spell – the only spell – that I've got. Put it on.' The king grumbled a bit more, but eventually he did what he was told.

The next day, as he rode through his kingdom, the few of his subjects who glanced up at him were filled with surprise. They had never seen the king smile before. And after a few days, a few of the bolder ones began to smile a small smile back at him instead of scurrying away. A week or so later, one very brave old woman actually stood upright, smiled at him and said in a loud voice, 'Good day, your majesty.' This surprised the king so much that he just didn't know what to say in return. But he didn't grumble mean things at her.

Word began to spread that the king had had a change of heart. People began to stand where they would be able to see him for themselves as he rode by. They would bow and then look up and smile at him. 'Ah,' thought the king, 'this is how a king should be treated. The magic mask is working. My subjects are becoming nicer people. They're not half as rotten as they used to be.'

From then on, things only got better. Each day more and more people spoke to the king, smiled and waved as he rode by. And the king started to wave back and even to shout his own greetings, 'Good morning' and 'How do you do?' In response, the people relaxed enough to tell him how life was for them. As the king heard their sad stories of struggle, poverty and illness, he made it his responsibility to arrange for his people to receive more food, medical help and other provisions, and, where it was needed, to ensure that disputes among them were settled fairly. And as he did all this, the people not only came to celebrate him but, in turn, he came to love them, really love them, because they had become so lovable.

All this, however, made the king feel increasingly guilty. He had come to care so much about these people now that he felt terrible he was manipulating their feelings for him by using the magic mask. Eventually, although the 100 days were not quite up, he knew he had to remove the mask; even if, as a result, the spell was broken and his people no longer loved him, at least he would have had these past days. Whatever the outcome, he knew that he could no longer continue to fool the people he had come to love.

So, standing in front of one of the rather large mirrors in the palace, he took one last long look at the mask on his face with its huge but fake smile, shut his eyes, reached up, and peeled it off. But when finally he mustered the courage to open his eyes and look into the mirror again at his real, mean, ugly, contorted face, a strange thing had happened. He saw another piece of magic – even more impressive than the mask had been. In the days he had come to love his people, his face had changed, and now, somehow, it matched the mask in every respect. It had a huge smile and looked as joyous as he felt about his people. He couldn't believe it. He wept and touched his laughing face.

The next morning when he went out among the people his heart was light for he knew he was being true to himself. He had somehow grown into a much better version of himself. And it is said that that king and the people of his kingdom lived, from that day forward, very fulfilled lives.

Notes

Prologue: The Geese

1. Based on a number of inter-related stories told by Søren Kierkegaard (1813–55), the Danish philosopher, theologian, poet, social critic and religious author. Kierkegaard wrote widely on the issues of the philosophy of religion, ethics and psychology, and made extensive use of parables and metaphors, for which geese became a favourite theme.
2. The phrase 'wild and precious' is found in 'The Summer Day', a poem by Mary Oliver in *New and Selected Poems* (Beacon Press, 2004).

Chapter 1: Wake Up!

1. *The Metro*, 29 July 2011; available at http://www.metro.co.uk/news/870785-mum-aged-32-woke-up-thinking-she-was-15#ixzz1UjSFgTUn.
2. Rabbi Meshulam Zusha of Hanipol (1718–1800).
3. The youth club I went to was held at Holmesdale Baptist Church in South Norwood, South London, and the route

I took home was up Dixon Road to Whitehorse Lane, where I lived with my parents, sisters and brother. I used to attend the Sunday school there as a child, but had reached the age where, a year or so beforehand, I'd abandoned church as not for me.

4. It was in response to this experience that I eventually began Oasis in 1985, which has now grown into a group of charities working to deliver housing, training, youth work, healthcare, family support, community churches, and primary, secondary and higher education. We currently work in ten countries around Europe, Asia, Africa and North America. For more see www.oasisuk.org.
5. IQ (Intelligence Quotient), EQ (Emotional Quotient) and SQ (Spiritual Quotient). More on all this later.

Chapter 2: Lift that Lid

1. Recounted with the permission of Jill Rowe, Oasis Ethos and Formation Director, who tells this story far more passionately than I can write it.
2. From Richard Rohr, *Falling Upward: A Spirituality for the Two Halves of Life* (Jossey-Bass, 2011).
3. John Maxwell wrote about the law of the lid in his book *The 21 Irrefutable Laws of Leadership* (Thomas Nelson, 1998), explaining that there is a self-imposed lid on a person's leadership ability which determines their level of effectiveness.
4. Watch the video at http://www.youtube.com/watch?v=BND6oxoRV3Y.

Chapter 3: The Big Story

1. For a further and really thought-provoking discussion of what Christianity is and isn't I recommend that you find yourself a copy of Francis Spufford's *Unapologetic: Why, Despite Everything, Christianity Can Still Make Surprising Emotional Sense* (Harper One, 2013).
2. 'I have come that they may have life, and have it to the full' (John 10:10).
3. The term 'Christian' appears in Acts 11:26, Acts 26:28 and 1 Peter 4:16.
4. See Genesis 5:24, 6:9; Isaiah 1:11–14; Amos 5:21–23 and Micah 6:8.
5. Isaiah 30:21.
6. John 14:6. The italics are mine.
7. Acts 9:2, 19:9, 23, 22:4, 24:14, 22.
8. See, for instance, Isaiah 66:13: 'As a mother comforts her child, so will I comfort you; and you will be comforted over Jerusalem.'
9. Perhaps, rather than God being more present in a church building or temple of some description, their value lies in the fact that we visit these places more open to the moment and therefore to the reality of the divine presence.
10. Although Jesus never talked to people about becoming a Christian, the Gospels record twenty-three occasions on which Jesus spoke about following him. Because a number of the references are duplicate stories, all in all these references relate to Jesus' use of the idea on sixteen different occasions: Matthew 4:19, 8:22, 9:9, 10:38, 16:24, 19:21,

19:28; Mark 1:17, 2:14, 8:34, 10:21; Luke 5:27, 9:23, 9:59, 14:27, 18:22; John 1:43, 8:12, 10:27, 12:26, 13:36, 21:19, 21:22.

Chapter 4: Punching Holes

1. Robert Louis Stevenson was best known for his novels *Treasure Island*, *Kidnapped* and *The Strange Case of Dr Jekyll and Mr Hyde*.
2. Matthew 6:9–10.
3. The kingdom of God (Gk: *basileia tou Theou*) and its equivalent, the kingdom of heaven (Gk: *basileia tōn ouranōn*), is one of the central elements of Jesus' teaching in the New Testament and is used by him in the Gospels of Matthew, Mark and Luke. The term 'kingdom of heaven' only occurs in Matthew, who also uses the term 'kingdom of God' on a handful of occasions. There is general agreement among scholars that the original term used by Jesus himself would have been 'kingdom of God' and that Matthew's use of the term 'kingdom of heaven' is a parallel which carries exactly the same meaning.
4. Jesus only used the term 'church' (Gk: *ekklésia*) on two occasions – both recorded in Matthew's Gospel (Matthew 16:17–19 and 18:15–17). However, the Gospels record Jesus talking about 'the kingdom' over one hundred times.
5. Matthew 6:33.
6. Luke 17:21.
7. This idea is what the theologians refer to as 'Inaugurated Eschatology' – the kingdom of God is both 'now and not yet', present and still future; though it has broken into the present through the ongoing work of Jesus, its ultimate fulfilment still lies in the future.

8. 1 John 4:8: 'Whoever does not love does not know God, because God is love.'
9. In Hebrew, the title 'God Almighty' is written as *El Shaddai* and probably means 'God, the All-powerful One', although there is a question among the majority of Bible scholars as to its precise meaning. We are first introduced to this name in Genesis 17:1, when God appears to Abram and says, 'I am God Almighty; walk before me faithfully and be blameless.' Understood in this context, the title speaks of the fact that this god is 'The God' of everything as opposed to 'a god' among many, rather than being a statement about absolute control over all events.
10. Traditionally the three Abrahamic religions (Judaism, Christianity and Islam) have attributed omnipotence (unlimited power) to God.
11. Ephesians 6:12.
12. To put this theologically, our ethics and values should all be eschatological choices. (*Eschatology* – from the Greek *eschatos*, meaning 'last', and *–logy*, meaning 'the study of'.) Eschatology is the part of theology concerned with the ultimate destiny of humanity. Christian and Jewish eschatologies view the end times as the consummation or perfection of God's creation of the universe.
13. Charles Jennens, a wealthy landowner with musical and literary interests, worked with Handel on various projects. In July 1741 Jennens sent Handel a new libretto for an oratorio and, in a letter dated 10 July to his friend Edward Holdsworth, wrote: 'I hope [Handel] will lay out his whole genius and skill upon it, that the composition may excell all his former compositions, as the subject excells every other subject. The subject is Messiah.'

14. Ivan Illich (1926–2002) was an Austrian philosopher, Roman Catholic priest and social critic who was particularly interested in the practice of education.

Chapter 5: Seeing is Believing

1. Greek τέλος.
2. The *Nicomachean Ethics* is Aristotle's best-known ethical work. It consists of ten books that were originally separate, which are thought to be based on notes from his lectures at the school he set up (known as the Lyceum), which were either compiled or edited by Nicomachus, his son. The theme of *Nicomachean Ethics* is a response to Socrates' great question that had previously been explored by Plato (Plato had been Socrates' student and became Aristotle's teacher): how should men best live? At the heart of Aristotle's unique contribution to this debate was his insistence that any study of ethics must be practical rather than merely theoretical. It must be more than an intellectual contemplation of good living but instead lead to the real end (*telos*) of actually living well (*eudaimōnia*).
3. Aristotle used the Greek word *arête*.
4. Aristotle used the Greek word *hexis*, which can also be translated into English as 'condition' or 'disposition'. *Hexis* was translated into Latin as *habitus* and then into English as 'habit'.
5. From the 1979 album *Slow Train Coming*.
6. Steve Turner, *The Gospel According to the Beatles* (Westminster: John Knox Press, 2006).
7. Greek, Roman and Norse paganism, for instance, provided

a way to acknowledge the power of the impulses that we struggle with both internally and externally, by turning them into capitalised Powers. Polytheistic (multi-god) religions separate out human passions, and then personify them into mythological figures who embody a particular trait. In this way the pagan pantheons supplied their worshippers with a kind of pack of cards – there was always one that suited the mood, the desire and the occasion.

8. From an interview with Muhammad Yunus on BBC Radio 4's *The World this Weekend* in early 2012. Yunus is an economist and founder of the Grameen Bank, which provides microcredit (small loans to poor people possessing no collateral) to help its clients establish creditworthiness and financial self-sufficiency. In 2006 Yunus and Grameen received the Nobel Peace Prize 'for their efforts through microcredit to create economic and social development from below'.

9. 'In each era since we turned away from the Bible's God, our culture has been shaped by one or more "god-substitutes" . . . They're the things that "matter most" to us, the principles that dominate our lives, determining our sense of what's important and the sources we look to for truth and meaning, for the understanding of right and wrong.' Pete Lowman, *A Long Way East of Eden: Could God Explain the Mess We're In?* (Carlisle: Paternoster, 2006), 257.

10. In ancient times, just like now, the primary teachers of morals were storytellers. The stories they told encompassed everything: the origin of the world, how peoples and communities came into being, the rules and boundaries that determined society, the way to teach children ideas about love, life and death, and how to be a good member of a commu-

nity. Ancient storytellers, such as Aesop, famous for his fables, knew that a well-crafted story is a more powerful tool in terms of moral formation than any textbook on ethical theory.

11. I got this insight from the wise and well-known theologian Lesslie Newbigin. In the last years of his life Lesslie lost his sight. I used to visit and read to him. But he used to say that despite his disability, like us all, he still wore spectacles – a big pair of cultural spectacles – that determined what he could 'see' and what he was blind to.
12. You can watch this advert at http://www.youtube.com/watch?v=6_WAmt3cMdk.

Chapter 6: Rekindling Imagination

1. Proverbs 29:18. Webster's Bible Translation
2. I remember being in trouble often as a child for daydreaming. But though I didn't realise it at the time, I was perhaps doing some of my best work.
3. Francis Spufford, *Unapologetic: Why, Despite Everything, Christianity Can Still Make Surprising Emotional Sense* (Faber & Faber, 2013).
4. In *How to be a Bad Christian . . . and a Better Human Being* (Hodder & Stoughton, 2012).

Chapter 7: The Story that Shapes Us

1. The text of the inscriptions was compiled from card indexes, which were drawn up shortly after the war on the basis of extant transport papers, registration lists and survivors'

accounts. The names of Holocaust victims, together with their dates of birth and death, are inscribed on all the interior walls. Where the precise date of death is not known, which is generally the case, the date of deportation to the ghettos and extermination camps in the east is stated instead – which is usually the last information available on the victims. Their names are arranged according to the towns and villages where they were living prior to deportation or arrest and are presented in alphabetical order.
2. Deuteronomy 11:18, 19.
3. Genesis 12:2–3. Equally, an over-'nationalistic' misunderstanding of this very text has played its part in the ongoing tragedy of the contemporary struggle between Israelis and Palestinians. A long-term internationally negotiated reconciliation process has, so far, failed to create real peace.
4. The first set of five Nobel prizes was awarded on the fifth anniversary of Alfred's death, on 10 December 1901. Today, six prizes – in 1968 an economics prize was added – continue to be awarded every year to those who make a marked contribution for the benefit of humanity.

Chapter 8: A New Agenda

1. Dave Tomlinson, *How to be a Bad Christian: and a Better Human Being* (Hodder & Stoughton, 2012), 209.
2. Anthony T. Kronman, *Education's End: Why Our Colleges and Universities Have Given Up on the Meaning of Life* (Yale University Press, 2005).
3. Kronman notes that America's colleges were originally set up as small institutions with strong religious roots who

regarded one of their greatest roles to be that of helping their students explore the big questions of vocation and purpose. But after the Civil War, educators were influenced by the ideas of the European Enlightenment and, as a consequence, colleges started to transform into institutions for research. With this growing focus on empirical research and the accompanying trend towards secularism, the space for students to grapple with life's biggest issues was lost. Indeed, it came to be seen as altogether inappropriate for an academic institution to meddle in these questions. Kronman however, believes that there would be great value in redressing the balance. Anthony Kronman, 'Why are we here? Colleges ignore life's biggest questions, and we all pay pay the price'; http://www.boston.com/news/globe/ideas/articles/2007/09/16/why_are_we_here/?page=full

4. Paul Vallely, 'Tough lessons: How teachers are seeking answers at Auschwitz', in *The Independent* (Sunday, 5 September 2010).
5. In reality, of course, science always has a level of doubt built into it. The most accurate definition of science is probably 'science is the least wrong thing that we currently believe'.
6. The German rocket scientist Wernher von Braun (1912–77) was the leading figure in the development of rocket technology. As a young man he became a member of the Nazi party and was commissioned as an SS officer. He was the central figure in Germany's rocket programme, responsible for designing and building the V-2 combat rocket which was used, to deadly effect, against Allied targets during the closing stages of the Second World War. However, at the end of the

war, von Braun surrendered to the United States military, rather than be captured by the advancing Soviets or shot dead by the Nazis to prevent his capture. Along with him, a team of 125 other German engineers were taken to the USA. There, von Braun worked for the American army, first on the development of a mid-range, and later an intercontinental, nuclear missile, before being transferred with his colleagues to work for the newly formed NASA. Here, he was appointed as the director of the Marshall Space Flight Center and led the development of the Saturn V booster rocket that was to propel the Apollo spacecraft into space and, in July 1969, eventually land the first men on the moon.

7. Maslow (1908–70) originally published his ideas in a paper entitled 'A Theory of Human Motivation' in 1943. However, his theory of self-actualisation was not fully expressed until his 1954 book *Motivation and Personality.* Maslow claimed that the higher levels of psychological development could only be achieved when all the lower needs were fulfilled. Indeed, 'self-actualization . . . rarely happens . . . certainly in less than 1% of the adult population'. Most of us, he concluded, were condemned to 'function most of the time on a level lower than that of self-actualization'.
8. Frank G. Goble, *The Third Force: The Psychology of Abraham Maslow* (New York, 1970), 25.
9. Howard Gardner, *Frames of Mind: The Theory of Multiple Intelligences* (Basic Books, 1983).
10. Danah Zohar, *Rewiring the Corporate Brain: Using the New Science to Rethink How We Structure and Lead Organizations* (Berrett-Koehler, 1997).
11. Frances Vaughan, *What is Spiritual Intelligence?* In *Journal*

of Humanistic Psychology 42:2 (Sage Publications, Spring 2002), 16–33.
12. Howard Gardner developed the theory of multiple intelligences, but did not include Spiritual Intelligence as one of them. Instead, he introduced the concept of 'Existential Intelligence'. However, he added that 'an explicit concern with spiritual or religious matters would be one variety – often the most important variety – of an Existential Intelligence'. Howard Gardner, *Intelligence Reframed: Multiple Intelligences for the 21st Century* (Basic Books, 1999), 53.
13. Stephen Covey, *The 8th Habit: From Effectiveness to Greatness* (Simon & Schuster, 2004), 53.
14. *Metanoia* is a compound word consisting of the preposition *meta* (after, with) and the verb *noeo* (to perceive, to think or to observe) – hence 'to think differently after'.
15. For more on this see N. T. Wright, *The Challenge of Jesus* (SPCK, 2000), 26.

Chapter 9: Life is Not an Exam

1. Technically known as 'deontological ethics', from Greek *deon*, meaning 'obligation' or 'duty'.
2. This approach is known as 'Consequentialism' (one famous form of which is 'Utilitarianism' – whose goal is 'the greatest good, for the greatest number of people for the greatest length of time').
3. The approach we've already talked about, first set out by Aristotle and technically known as 'Virtue Ethics'.
4. Though, of course, there is no universal agreement on what this list should consist of.

5. Exodus 20. The fourth commandment says: 'You shall not bear false witness.'
6. Here's an interesting question: Why did Jesus never write, or dictate, a book of detailed rules on how to live?
7. This is clear from the way in which the commandments are introduced by a preamble, which sets them in context. 'I am the Lord your God, who brought you out of Egypt, out of the land of slavery' (Exodus 20:2).
8. See Exodus, Leviticus and Deuteronomy.
9. See Exodus 21:24, Leviticus 24:20–22 and Deuteronomy 19:21.
10. See Luke 2:41–49.
11. This man would have been an expert in Jewish law, as contained in the Pentateuch, and in its interpretation.
12. The first of these two principles was taken from Deuteronomy 6:5 (the chapter after the Ten Commandments) and the second from Leviticus 19:18.
13. Hearing that Jesus had silenced the Sadducees, the Pharisees got together. One of them, an expert in the law, tested him with this question: 'Teacher, which is the greatest commandment in the Law?' Jesus replied: '"Love the Lord your God with all your heart and with all your soul and with all your mind." This is the first and greatest commandment. And the second is like it: "Love your neighbour as yourself." All the Law and the Prophets hang on these two commandments' (Matthew 22:34–40).
14. On this point, read Jesus' parable of the Good Samaritan in Luke 10:25–37. Our task is to grapple constantly with what it means to recognise our neighbour and to love them

as we love ourselves. When a teacher of the law asks Jesus 'Who is my neighbour?' Jesus replies with the story of the Good Samaritan. This is a strange answer. The teacher of the law had asked who his neighbour was; Jesus' reply was to explain how to be a good neighbour by answering a subtly different and far more socially and politically challenging question, 'To whom can I be a neighbour?' The implication of the story is that there is no one who is not our neighbour; no one to whom we should not show grace and mercy.

15. However, the other day in a shopping centre, I heard a mother command her daughter, 'Don't trust anybody.'

Chapter 10: Throw Out the Rule Book

1. 'Contextualism' (or Situation ethics) – 'The right thing to do depends on the situation' – sometimes rather unfairly caricatured as 'If it feels good, do it', is a recent cousin of Consequentialism. Consequentialist approaches to ethics are said to date back to Mozi (470–391 BC), the Chinese philosopher who founded Mohism. Mohism's approach to ethical decisions was to seek to find the solution which did the maximum good and caused the minimum pain. Another influential form of Consequentialism, known as Utilitarianism, was founded by Jeremy Bentham, the British thinker (1748–1832) and also taught by John Stuart Mill (1806–73). All are underpinned by the view that there are no universal moral rules or rights – each case is unique and deserves a unique solution.
2. From N. T. Wright, *Virtue Reborn* (SPCK, 2010).

3. 'Take the Waiting out of Wanting' was an advertising slogan for Access credit cards.
4. Police investigations into the phone-hacking scandal eventually led to various high-profile resignations, a number of arrests, several court cases and, to date, one conviction. In July 2011, David Cameron, the British Prime Minister, also announced the setting up of a large-scale public inquiry, headed by Lord Justice Leveson, whose job it would be to probe the phone-hacking scandal and the behaviour of the press. In 2014 the new Independent Press Standards Organisation (IPSO) was established to regulate the UK's newspapers and magazines. However, although the IPSO is 'independent', its members are nominated from the print industry, which has already raised a debate over whether it will have the teeth to bring about lasting change to the culture and ethics of the British press.
5. Speaking at the MacTaggart Lecture at the Edinburgh International Television Festival in 2012; http://www.guardian.co.uk/media/2012/aug/23/elisabeth-murdoch-mactaggart-lecture.
6. From 'Money: A Crisis of Value', Tuesday, 6 October 2009, St Paul's Cathedral. Available from http://www.stpaulsinstitute.org.uk.

Chapter 11: In Pursuit of Excellence

1. David Shenk in the RSA journal. David is author of *The Genius in All of Us: Why Everything You've Been Told About Genetics, Talent, and IQ is Wrong* (Icon Books, 2010).

2. Matthew Syed, *Bounce: The Myth of Talent and the Power of Practice* (Fourth Estate, 2011).
3. http://www.golfdigest.com/magazine/myshot_gd0210#ixzz1UoXnmMM7.
4. http://www.lvbeethoven.com/Bio/BiographyLudwig.html.
5. Jamie Wilson, 'Librarian finds lost Beethoven score in dusty cabinet', in the *Guardian* (Friday, 14 October 2005); http://www.guardian.co.uk/world/2005/oct/14/usa.arts.
6. Matthew Syed, *Bounce.*
7. Esther de Waal, *A Life-Giving Way: A Commentary on the Rule of St Benedict* (Collegeville: The Liturgical Press, 1995), 17.
8. Hebrews 2:17–18: '[Jesus] had to be made like them, fully human in every way . . . Because he himself suffered when he was tempted, he is able to help those who are being tempted.'
9. Dallas Willard, *The Divine Conspiracy* (Fount, 1998), 388.

Chapter 12: Learning the Hard Way

1. As Armstrong stepped off the Apollo Lunar Module and onto the surface of the moon, he delivered these famous words: 'That's one small step for [a] man, one giant leap for mankind' and ever since the debate has raged. Did Armstrong say 'a man' or just 'man'? If you listen to any of the recordings of the transmission, there is no 'a' before 'man'. At first, Armstrong insisted he had said 'a man' and the 'a' must have been obscured by static, though eventually, after listening to the various recordings many times, he admitted he must have dropped it by mistake.

However, it has since been claimed that modern digital audio analysis of the original recordings reveals the presence of the missing 'a' and that Armstrong did, in fact, say 'a man'!

2. Info from http://www.huffingtonpost.com/2012/08/25/apollo-11-neil-armstrong_n_1830571.html and an extract from Andrew Smith, *Moondust: In Search of the Men Who Fell to Earth* (Bloomsbury, 2005), reproduced in *The Week* (September 2012).
3. In the English-speaking world, the word 'discipline' often gets muddled and confused with the concepts of 'wrongdoing', 'anger', 'punishment' and 'restriction' rather than associated with training, development and freedom. So, for instance, when a parent speaks of 'disciplining' their child, we automatically assume they have told them off, grounded them, removed their pocket money . . . or something worse still. The very etymology of the word *discipline*, however, should point us in an entirely different direction. Discipline is derived from the Latin word *disciplina*, which means 'instruction given to a disciple', but even the *Oxford Pocket Dictionary* blurs this. It has, as its first definition of discipline, 'the practice of training people to obey rules or a code of behaviour, using punishment to correct disobedience'.

Chapter 13: Get Wired

1. *Evan Almighty* (Universal Pictures, 2007).
2. The factuality of this story is disputed by some – but, even so, the power of the illustration remains.

3. Philippians 2:13.
4. 2 Corinthians 3:18, New Living Translation (NLT).
5. The word 'inspire' comes from the Latin *inspirare*, which literally means 'to breathe or blow into', being comprised of *in*, meaning 'into', and *spirare*, meaning 'breathe'.
6. See Norman Doidge, *The Brain that Changes Itself: Stories of Personal Triumph from the Frontiers of Brain Science* (Penguin, 2008).
7. Stephen Covey, the great leadership guru, famously talked about the four stages of learning and mastering any skill:

   Stage One: 'Unconscious incompetence' – that happy state of total ignorance when you are so incompetent that you don't even realise how incompetent you are.
   Stage Two: 'Conscious incompetence' – the depressing moment when the truth dawns and you first become aware of what it is that you don't know and how boxed-in that makes you.
   Stage Three: 'Conscious competence' – the painful and long process of struggling to get to grips with what it is that you don't know or can't do.
   Stage Four: 'Unconscious competence' – the Eureka moment when you realise that you're now so familiar with what you once didn't know how to do that it's become second nature and you do it quite naturally.

   Perhaps the most overwhelmingly depressing moment in this cycle, whatever the skill that we are trying to learn, is that of conscious incompetence – when we are first awoken to the reality of our ineptitude. However, this deeply uncomfortable moment is always our friend, never our enemy – because without it we would never recognise our need to grow.

8. http://www.nadalvsfederer.com/us-open-serve-speed-stats-2011/.
9. http://www.wellcome.ac.uk/About-us/75th-anniversary/WTVM052023.htm.

Chapter 14: Putting it On

1. http://www.bbc.co.uk/sport/0/olympics/19174302.
2. The Buddha, *Dhammapada*, Verse 80.
3. Benedict's first community was a monastery at Monte Cassino. Still today, Benedictine communities around the world base their life together on his *Rule of Life*.
4. Matthew 22:36–40.
5. Ephesians 4:22–26, 28–29, 31–32, emphasis added.
6. Colossians 3:8–10, 11–14, emphasis added.
7. A candy stick with the name Brighton written all the way through it.

Chapter 15: A Counter-revolutionary Life

1. And for his influential book *The Politics of Jesus* (Eerdmans, 1972).
2. Aristotle's nine intellectual virtues are *sophia* (wisdom), *episteme* (scientific knowledge), *nous* (intelligence, intuition or common sense), *phronesis* (prudence), *technē* (practical or

technical skill), *euboulia* (resourcefulness), *sunesis* (astuteness), *gnomē* (good judgement) and *deinotes* (cleverness).

His nine moral virtues include *andreia* (courage), *sōphrosunē* (temperance), *eleutheriotēs* (liberality), *megaloprepeia* (magnificence), *megalopsuchia* (magnanimity/benevolence/greatness of soul), *praotēs* (patience/gentleness), *alētheia* (truthfulness/sincerity), *eutrapelos* (wittiness or charm) and *philia* (friendliness/civility).

Aristotle also discusses three other character traits, although he does this without ever giving them a name:

> *Proper ambition/pride:* He discusses the two vices associated with too much pride or too little pride, but explains that there is no word in the Greek language to describe the correct balance.
>
> *Modesty*: Once again he does not have a word to sum his thoughts up on this; instead, he makes the argument that a sense of shame is not a virtue and is to be avoided without falling into the trap of an exaggerated sense of pride.
>
> *Righteous indignation/just resentment*: He discusses, at length – Book V of *Nicomachean Ethics* is entirely given over to it – the issue of justice and fairness, and concludes that a man should have a proper sense of indignation at a lack of justice and fairness.

3. Aristotle's account of the virtues is all to do with the role of men, never that of women.

Now the man is thought to be proud who thinks himself

worthy of great things, being worthy of them . . . The proud man, then, is the man we have described. For he who is worthy of little and thinks himself worthy of little is temperate, but not proud; for pride implies greatness . . . On the other hand, he who thinks himself worthy of great things, being unworthy of them, is vain; though not everyone who thinks himself worthy of more than he really is worthy of is vain. The man who thinks himself worthy of less than he is really worthy of is unduly humble . . . If, then, he deserves and claims great things, and above all the great things, he will be concerned with one thing in particular . . . and this is honour . . . Such, then, is the proud man; the man who falls short of him is unduly humble, and the man who goes beyond him is vain. Pride, then, is concerned with honour on the grand scale, as has been said. *The Nicomachean Ethics of Aristotle Book IV*

4. See Alasdair MacIntyre's seminal work *After Virtue: A Study in Moral Theory* (University of Notre Dame Press, 1981) for a discussion of this.
5. In the first generation of Titans, the males were Oceanus, Hyperion, Coeus, Cronus, Crius and Lapetus, and the females (the 'Titanesses') were Mnemosyne, Tethys, Theia, Phoebe, Rhea and Themis. The second generation of Titans consisted of Hyperion's children Eos, Helios and Selene; Coeus's daughters Leto and Asteria; Lapetus's sons Atlas, Prometheus, Epimetheus and Menoetius; Oceanus's daughter Metis; and Crius' sons Astraeus, Pallas and Perses.
6. From Plutarch's (*c.* AD 46–120) *Life of Alexander*.
7. What makes a leader great? Collins says that truly great

leaders – Level 5 Leaders – are humble people. They don't seek success for their own glory; rather, success is necessary so that the team and organisation can thrive. They share credit for success, and they're the first to accept blame for mistakes. They may not be in your face, loud and larger than life, but they are fearless when it comes to making tough decisions and taking what others may consider huge risks for the good of those they serve. Collins explains that a Level 5 Leader will also have the skills of levels 1, 2, 3 and 4 people:

Level 1: 'A Highly Capable Individual' has useful levels of knowledge, the talent and skills needed to do a good job and makes high-quality contributions with their work.
Level 2: 'A Contributing Team Member', using their knowledge and skills, works effectively, productively and successfully with others to help them succeed.
Level 3: 'A Competent Manager' is able to organise a group effectively to achieve specific goals and objectives.
Level 4: 'An Effective Leader' is able to galvanise a department or organisation to meet performance objectives and achieve a vision. Collins says that this is the category that the majority of competent company leaders fall into.
Level 5: 'A Great Leader' has all of the abilities needed for the other four levels, plus the unique blend of humility and will that is required for true greatness.

8. The concept of a 'Level 5 Leader' came about during the late 1990s through a study that Collins began concerning the question of what makes a great company. He started by looking at 1,435 companies, and ended up whittling that

number down to 11 which he believed were truly 'great'. These were all headed by what he termed 'Level 5 Leaders'. In 2001 he published his best-selling book *Good to Great: Why Some Companies Make the Leap . . . and Others Don't* (HarperBusiness, 2001) in which he set out his ideas.

9. Hitler drew on Nietzsche's ideas, often visited the Nietzsche museum in Weimar and publicised his veneration for the philosopher by posing for photographs of himself staring in rapture at the bust of the great man. Without doubt, however, Hitler misunderstood, misinterpreted and perverted Nietzsche's thought as well as ignoring much in it that was hostile to his aims.

   Nietzsche is known for his use of poetry and prose (sometimes together in poetic prose style) in his writings. And even today, because of this evocative and loose way of writing, his work remains controversial and continues to generate varying interpretations and misinterpretations.

   In 1889, this problem was exacerbated when, aged forty-four, Nietzsche, already plagued by ill health (syphilis and constant prolonged bouts of migraine), also suffered a serious mental breakdown from which he never recovered. He lived the rest of his life in care, with his mother until her death in 1897, after which this responsibility fell to his sister Elisabeth Förster-Nietzsche.

   At this point, Elisabeth, who was married to Bernhard Förster (a well-known German nationalist and anti-Semitist), assumed the role of editor of her brother's manuscripts and reworked all his unpublished writings to fit with her husband's ideology. This was often done in ways that were contrary to Nietzsche's stated opinions. He was actually strongly and explicitly opposed to both anti-Semitism and nationalism. Through Förster-Nietzsche's editions, however, Nietzsche's name became associated with German militarism and Nazism. Although Nietzsche died in 1900, Elisabeth continued to publish his work for some years.

10. G. K. Chesterton, *What's Wrong with the World* (Dover Publications, 2007).

Chapter 16: A Different Kind of Vision

1. Galatians 5:22–23. Several insights emerge from using the term 'fruit' for virtues. One is to show how these must grow from within rather than being externally imposed. Another is that they are linked together: if you want one of them, work at developing them all. If you are learning to ride a bicycle, the skill is mastering the use of the pedals, the handlebars, the gears, the brakes and the bell, as well as learning how to perch on the saddle and keep your balance, all at the same time. Conquering one or two of these, while neglecting the rest, will leave you sitting in the gutter.
2. The Greek word that Paul uses, *agápē* (ἀγάπη), is often translated as 'unconditional love'.
3. 1 Corinthians 1:20, 22–24.
4. 1 Corinthians 13:1–8, 13.
5. 1 Peter 2:7, quoting Psalm 118:22.
6. Jürgen Moltmann, *The Crucified God: The Cross of Christ as the Foundation and Criticism of Christian Theology* (Fortress Press, 1972).
7. C. S. Lewis, *The Four Loves* (Geoffrey Bles, 1960).

8. Václav Havel (1936–2011) was a Czech playwright, essayist, poet, dissident and politician. Havel served as the last president of Czechoslovakia (1989–92) and the first president of the Czech Republic (1993–2003). Havel was voted fourth in *Prospect* magazine's 2005 global poll of the world's top 100 intellectuals.
9. Philippians 2:6–9.
10. Matthew 5:39.
11. This, of course, is still true in some traditional cultures today.
12. Matthew 26:52.

Chapter 17: The Indelible Image

1. http://oxforddictionaries.com.
2. Genesis 1:27.
3. The first chapter of Genesis, just like the rest of the texts that make up the Bible, was not written as a thesis to be debated by the academics of the day, but rather to bring hope and encouragement to ordinary people as they learnt its story or heard it read. For more on this read Stanley J. Grenz, *The Social God and the Relational Self* (Westminster John Knox Press, 2001).
4. Genesis 1 is a piece of poetry. The majority of scholars are convinced that it was originally written with a liturgical purpose for use by the Jewish community in public worship – something akin to what we would know as a responsive reading. Unfortunately, however, it has often been misrepresented as an historical narrative or a scientific account. The result of this misunderstanding has been, for those

involved, to create a false schism between the disciplines of science and theology, which, as we know, has done huge damage to the credibility of the Bible over the last century.

The Genesis 1 account was never written as an historical record of 'how' God created the world, but is rather a beautiful poem explaining the 'why' and 'who' behind it all. Its theme is 'The Big Plan' rather than 'The Big Bang' and it sits happily, side by side, with a modern understanding of the science of the first seconds of the universe. As one old rabbi once commented to a student who asked him if the Genesis 1 creation story was as true as their latest science textbook: 'Oh no. It is much truer than that.'

5. D. J. A. Clines, 'The Image of God in Man', in *Tyndale Bulletin* 19 (1968), 55–103.
6. Gerhard von Rad, *Genesis: A Commentary*, trans. John Marks (Westminster, 1973).
7. Gordon Wenham, *Genesis 1–15*, Vol. 1 of the *Word Biblical Commentary*, ed. David A. Hubbard, Glenn W. Barker and John D. W. Watts (Word, 1987).
8. *Imago Dei* is Latin for 'image of God' and has come to be used as the theological term to denote the nature of the relationship between God and humanity.
9. The *Enuma Elish* (commonly known as the Babylonia Creation Story) recounts the struggle between cosmic order and chaos. It is one of many creation stories or 'myths' from various ancient cultures that have now been rediscovered. There are too many similarities between the Genesis 1 account and *Enuma Elish* to deny any relationship between them, and most scholars believe that the Babylonian story predates the biblical account. Because of this, some historians have

concluded that Genesis is simply a rewriting of the Babylonian story. However, for all the similarities, there are a whole set of very significant differences as well. Though the Genesis narrative freely draws on the same metaphors and symbolism as *Enuma Elish*, it does so in order to subvert and correct what it sees as false understandings with its own distinctive theology or 'knowledge' about the one true God – the Creator of all.

10. Among biblical scholars, by far the most widely accepted interpretation of the Genesis creation account, both now and throughout church history, has been what is known as the 'literary theory', which seeks to ask what kind of literature the early chapters of Genesis are, and which, as a result, sees no schism between the disciplines of science and theology – both of which it seeks to take seriously. As long ago as AD 391, for instance, Augustine wrote a commentary on Genesis in which he said that, in his view, the 'days' of creation were not literal but figurative.

The 'literary approach' hinges on a critical question: what kind of literature are the biblical creation stories? Is the whole Bible simply an historical narrative – one that just reports events how they happened? Of course, on reflection, we all acknowledge that the Bible contains lots of different forms of literature. History, poetry, prose, parable, prophecy, allegory, dreams and visions, etc. – all are present in the scriptures. For example, in the Psalms the Old Testament variously describes God as a rock, a fortress, a shepherd and a warrior, while the New Testament refers to Jesus as a door, a temple, a lion, a shepherd and a lamb.

Genesis 1 certainly reads more like poetry than history.

Each creative day starts with the phrase 'And God said' and each ends with 'And there was evening, and there was morning.' In fact as already stated the majority of scholars are convinced that it was originally written with a liturgical purpose for use by the Jewish community in public worship. The NIV translation of the Bible even lays out the story of the days-of-creation passage as a hymn or poem.

It is also of interest that when Darwin first published his famous book *On the Origin of Species* in 1859, Christians adopted differing views to it. While some, as is well known, were very suspicious, seeing its thesis as a threat to their faith as well as a challenge to the authority of the biblical text, many others welcomed it, and Darwin's friend, his local vicar, wrote the foreword for it.

11. Albert Einstein, quoted in 'Wit & Wisdom', *The Week* (13 November 2004).
12. Richard Dawkins, *River Out of Eden* (New York: Basic Books, 1995), 132.
13. Howard Peskett and Vinoth Ramachandra, *The Message of Mission* (IVP, 2003).
14. Genesis 2 and 3 – the story of Adam and Eve – comes from a different and separate story to the creation poem of Genesis 1. Much of our modern understanding of the separate Genesis creation accounts is derived from the work of Julius Wellhausen's 'documentary hypothesis'. It holds that the Torah or Pentateuch (the first five books of our modern Bible) was derived from what were originally independent and parallel narratives, which were subsequently combined into the current form by a series of redactors (editors).

During the eighteenth and nineteenth centuries, biblical scholars, using source criticism, developed the theory that the Torah was composed of texts which over time had been woven together from separate, independent documents. General agreement was reached around the view that there were four main sources which were combined into their final form by a series of editors (or redactors). These four sources came to be known as J (the Yahwist source – J is the German equivalent of the English letter Y); E (the Elohist source); D (the Deuteronomist source) and P (the Priestly source).

The German biblical scholar Julius Wellhausen (1844–1918) played a key role in this process and is particularly remembered for his work on ordering the four written sources chronologically in terms of the date of their authorship:

J – *c.* 950 BC in the southern kingdom of Judah.
E – *c.* 850 BC in the northern kingdom of Israel.
D – *c.* 600 BC in Jerusalem during a period of religious renewal.
P – *c.* 500 BC by Jewish priests in exile in Babylon.

Through the twentieth century, various important modifications to Wellhausen's work were introduced by further research, including its dating, the oral as opposed to written nature of some of the sources, etc. Over the last twenty-five years there has also been a proliferation of authorship theories (many of them radically different from Wellhausen's). However, much of the terminology and many of the insights of the original documentary hypothesis – notably its claim that the Pentateuch is the work of many hands and many centuries and that its final form is the work of redactors – continues to form the framework within which the origins of the Torah are discussed and debated.

15. This is seen by the use of the term in Genesis 5:1–2 and again in Genesis 9:6.
16. St Augustine, *Later Works, On The Trinity, Book XIV, The Perfection of the Image in the Contemplation of God*, edited by John Burnaby (Westminster John Knox Press, 1955), 103.
17. See the *Oasis Faithworks Charter*, which underpins all our work at www.oasisuk.org.
18. The Magnificat is recorded in Luke 1:46–55.
19. From an open letter written by my friend Stephen M. Ferguson. Used with his permission.

Chapter 18: The Elephant in the Room

1. Quoted by Francis Spufford in *Unapologetic*.
2. In the Ancient Near East the Bronze Age stretched from *c.* 3300–1200 BC and the Iron Age from *c.* 1200–500 BC.
3. 1 Samuel 15:3.
4. See Deuteronomy 24:17–22.
5. Leviticus 25:23.
6. See Deuteronomy 23:19.
7. Psalm 103:8 (New Living Translation). See also Psalm 30:5, 86:15 and 145:8–9.
8. The Code of Hammurabi, Laws 196–201.
9. Exodus 21:23–25.
10. Matthew 5:38–39.
11. Hebrews 1:1–3.

Chapter 19: The Sacred Library

1. On the one hand, we have all heard preachers imply that every syllable of the Bible is 'God's Word' and that it is as applicable today as it was when it was first penned, while, on the other, in spite of 2 Timothy 3:16's proclamation that 'All Scripture is God-breathed and is useful for teaching, rebuking, correcting and training in righteousness . . .', we sometimes wonder if it might be best to consign large chunks of it to a filing cabinet labelled 'no longer relevant'. However we understand 2 Timothy 3:16, it is important to recognise that, though these words are now often applied to the whole of the Christian Bible, in context the writer's original intention was not to regard his own writing as scripture and, of course, this comment was penned before what we now regard as the canon of the New Testament had been compiled. Thus, the reference is to the Jewish Bible – or what we know as the Old Testament – the very bit that so many have most problems with!
2. This belief comes in two slightly different versions: 'Biblical Infallibility' – that the Bible is incapable of error in matters of faith and practice, but not necessarily in historic or scientific matters; and 'Biblical Inerrancy' – that the Bible is without error in any aspect, spoken by God and written down in its perfect form by humans.
3. The Judaic and Islamic communities both face these same questions about how to read their sacred texts.
4. See Matthew 5:17.
5. I love Seth Godin's witty remark: 'We need heretics to keep faith alive. Heretics are the people of faith who will risk everything to challenge the prevailing religion of the day

. . . That's why real change . . . can only come from people with belief in the key mission and disrespect for the bureaucracy that has grown up over time.' Seth Godin, 'Tribes: We Need You to Lead Us', in *RSA Journal* (Summer 2009).

6. John 8:5.
7. RQ (Religious Quotient).
8. Numbers 15:32–36.
9. Exodus 20:8–10.
10. Jesus in Mark 2:23–27.
11. It seems to me that those who insist that the Old Testament's reporting of God as fierce, violent and the architect of a justice system filled with oppression and discrimination is an accurate portrayal of his character and actions (and therefore dismiss the idea that the writers of the text exhibit a limited understanding of God) are, in effect, saying that rather than humanity's ideas evolving, God's have!
12. The word Bible literally means 'the books' or 'library'.
13. For a much fuller treatment of this understanding of biblical interpretation see Karl Allan Kuhn, *Having Words with God: The Bible as Conversation* (Fortress Press, 2008).
14. There are several New Testament texts that are very clear about the role of women in Christian communities. 1 Timothy 2:12–14 says: 'I do not permit a woman to teach or to assume authority over a man; she must be quiet. For Adam was formed first, then Eve. And Adam was not the one deceived; it was the woman who was deceived and became a sinner.' The text appeals to Genesis 2 and the very nature of creation as its source of authority for the silence and submission of women.

In 1 Corinthians 14:34–35, Paul writes: 'Women should remain silent in the churches. They are not allowed to speak, but must be in submission, as the law says. If they want to enquire about something, they should ask their own husbands at home; for it is disgraceful for a woman to speak in the church.'

There have been numerous popular and theological attempts to soften these injunctions. Some suggest these verses were added by later editors, or that they address specific communities and refer to particular women. Others say they are offset by other passages. However, in truth, the absolute and universal character of the Epistles' instructions is not easy to escape: 'I do not permit a woman to teach or to assume authority over a man', 'for it is disgraceful for a woman to speak in the church' and 'Women should remain silent in the churches.'

15. Wilberforce and his friends were often known as the 'Clapham Sect' because a number of them lived in what was then the village of Clapham, south of London. It is interesting that, as important as the fight to end the cruelty of the slave trade within the British Empire was, it was just one part of a much wider battle against injustice and a programme for social and moral reform. The Clapham Sect, inspired by their deep faith in Christ, were also key players in working to set up a plethora of other campaigns on issues ranging from prison reform and education to poverty reduction and the prevention of cruelty to animals. Indeed, in 1800 alone, Wilberforce established campaigns on schooling for the poor and inoculation for children, as well as against bull baiting and Sunday trading.

16. E.g. Leviticus 25:44–46.
17. Although it is sometimes argued that Galatians 3:28 explains, 'There is neither Jew nor Gentile, neither slave nor free, nor is there male and female, for you are all one in Christ Jesus', this passage is no more a call for the abolition of slavery than it is of the sexes or of national identities and cultures. Aside from any other consideration, however, this lone verse in Galatians, written in the mid-first century (in the mid- to late 50s), predates both Ephesians (6:5: 'Slaves, obey your earthly masters . . .') and Colossians (3:22: 'Slaves, obey your earthly masters in everything . . .'), both of which were authored in the early 60s.

Chapter 20: Thirty Pieces of Silver

1. A famous paraphrase from volume five of Marcel Proust's monumental novel *À la recherche du temps perdu* (*In Search of Lost Time*), which was originally published in French in seven parts between 1913 and 1927.
2. Matthew 26:14–16.
3. The story is told in Matthew 27:1–7. However, there is a very different account of Judas's death, as told by Luke in Acts 1:15–19. Although some have tried to harmonise these accounts, it is an exceptionally difficult task!
4. For the whole account, see Matthew 16:13–28.
5. It is almost impossible to overestimate the honour, prestige and status of the role of Messiah in Jewish eyes. Just as we might expect our political leaders to sort out education, the health service and the economy, so the Jews expected the genuine Messiah to deliver on a number of fundamental

political issues, including, as they saw it, returning them fully from exile, which meant defeating Rome, bringing them independence and restoring the Temple. As the theologian and New Testament scholar N. T. Wright has pointed out, by achieving these goals any Jew might be accepted as Israel's Messiah.

The problem was that this hope of national deliverance had been frustrated for centuries. The Romans were just the most recent in a long line of foreign rulers who had left the Jewish people socially, culturally, politically and religiously ravaged. Time and again a leader had arisen from among the Jews intent on overthrowing, once and for all, their nation's enemies. But each time, sooner or later, these would-be Messiahs proved inadequate for the task, and the people's hopes were torn to shreds.

The closest the people of Israel had ever come to freedom was in 164 BC, when on 25 December, Judas Maccabaeus, along with a zealous band of accomplices, succeeded in ousting the tyrannical Syrian leader Antiochus Epiphanes and liberated the Temple, cleansing and reconsecrating it. For nearly one hundred years Israel enjoyed independence under the rule of the Hasmoneans (the Priest Kings). But tragically even this turned out simply to be a mere historical blip – a rare breath of freedom. By 63 BC, Rome had moved in, crushed whoever stood in their way and seized power. Judas Maccabaeus, so it turned out, was not the Messiah after all. That title was still to be handed out to the one who could bring lasting freedom to God's people.

6. Matthew 21:8–10.
7. Testament of Naphtali, 5.

8. See John 6:15.
9. Matthew 21:13.
10. Matthew 21:17.
11. Matthew 26:14–16.
12. Matthew 26:45–46.
13. Matthew 26:47–52.
14. Matthew 26:56.
15. I first came across this insight into Judas's motives in John Howard Yoder's book *The Politics of Jesus*, 47. There he explains that 'The hypothesis is not new that the intention of Judas was not to turn Jesus over to the authorities but rather that by his betrayal he might force Jesus, in order to defend himself, finally at the last minute to precipitate that holy war through which Judas the Zealot expected the breakthrough of the Kingdom of God to be achieved.'

Chapter 21: The Table of Friendship

1. After three days, the mountain fell silent and Pompeii lay lost and buried for nearly seventeen hundred years before its rediscovery in 1748. Ironically, the city was buried on the day following the festival of Vulcanalia, to honour Vulcan, the Roman god of fire and volcanoes. Vulcanalia was celebrated annually on 23 August, when the summer heat placed crops and granaries at greatest risk of burning. As part of this festival, live fish and small animals were thrown onto bonfires as sacrifices, to appease Vulcan and to win his favour.
2. Mark 14:22–26.
3. At the heart of this important issue is the question about the meaning of the term 'atonement' in the Old Testament.

In Leon Morris's classic text, *The Apostolic Preaching of the Cross* (Inter-Varsity Press, 1955), 121, he entitles the section on atonement in the Old Testament 'The problem of atonement'. In it he raises the question of the ambiguity of the term in its relationship to 'blood' – the giving and taking of life – recognising that 'In other places atonement is connected with such ceremonies as the pouring of oil on the head of the cleansed leper (Lv. 14:18, 29), the offering of incense (Nu. 16:46), the scapegoat (Lv. 16:10), and there are others.' He concludes that 'these do not seem to forward our inquiry so we pass over them . . .'. For two very insightful studies on the subject, see Joel Green and Mark Baker, *Recovering the Scandal of the Cross* (IVP, 2000) and Mark Green, ed., *Proclaiming the Scandal of the Cross* (Baker, 2006).

4. John 13:1–5.
5. John 13:12–18.
6. Matthew 20:28; Mark 10:45.
7. 1 Corinthians 11:17–22.
8. Charles Dickens, *A Christmas Carol* (Bradbury and Evans, 1858), 2.
9. I am indebted to Mike Starkey's book *Born to Shop* (Monarch, 1989) for some of the ideas in this chapter, in particular the previous two paragraphs.

Chapter 22: God in Disguise

1. In the Jewish Morning Prayer, which is still used by some communities even today, women substitute 'Blessed are You, O Lord our God, King of the Universe, who has not made me a woman' with 'Blessed are You, O Lord our God, King

of the Universe, that You made me according to Your will'.

2. In fact, on at least two occasions, the Old Testament also challenges the people of Israel to love the stranger or outsider. See Deuteronomy 10:19: 'And you are to love those who are foreigners, for you yourselves were foreigners in Egypt', and Leviticus 19:34: 'The foreigner residing among you must be treated as your native-born. Love them as yourself, for you were foreigners in Egypt. I am the Lord your God.'
3. Matthew 5:44–45.
4. Luke 10:25–37.
5. Way back in 722 BC.
6. For much more on the tensions between the Jews and the Samaritans see Mark A. Powell, *Introducing the New Testament: A Historical, Literary, and Theological Survey* (Baker Academic, 2009), Chapter 1: 'The People of Palestine at the Time of Jesus'.
7. All this was 'read out of' or, more accurately, 'read in to' Genesis 9:20–27.
8. Acts 17:26. The Areopagus was the High Court of Appeal in the city of Athens.
9. Matthew 25:31–46.

Chapter 23: Chance Your Arm

1. This story is found in the Book of Jubilees (an ancient – 150–100 BC – Jewish commentary on Genesis and part of Exodus, and considered part of the canon of the Bible by the Ethiopian Orthodox Church), and also in the Quran (Quran 6:75–79).
2. Modern-day Iraq.

3. The three monotheistic faiths – Judaism (the oldest), Christianity (the middle sibling) and Islam (the youngest) – all refer to the one true, universal, Creator God. Orthodox Jews avoid using the personal name of God (Hebrew יהוה – YHVH – Yahweh) and choose to use the term HaShem ('The Name') as a euphemism instead. Ho Theos – (Greek Ο Θεός – The God) is used frequently in the New Testament. And al-Lāh (Allāh), an Arabic word meaning 'The God', is used by Muslims, as well as by Arab Christians. Pope John Paul II referred to Jews as 'our elder brothers and sisters in faith'.
4. Very similar to the story of Shadrach, Meshach and Abednego in the Old Testament book of Daniel.
5. Genesis 12:1–5.
6. In doing so, Abram becomes the father of what we now call monotheism; the belief in the existence of one God of everyone and everything, as opposed to polytheism (many gods).
7. Genesis 17:5.
8. Judaism, Christianity and Islam all own this same story – this same vision: they are the three Abrahamic faiths. The challenge is: can we work together to fulfil it, or will we destroy one another?
9. Muhammad (570–632) unified Arabia into a single religious movement: Islam. Muslims consider him to be the restorer of the uncorrupted original monotheistic faith of Adam, Noah, Abraham, Moses, Jesus and other prophets.

   Muhammad was born and raised in the desert city of Mecca in Saudi Arabia in 570. He was deeply spiritual, and from an early age would spend many hours alone in prayer. In his quest for the one true God he developed the habit of retreating to a cave on Mount Hira, three miles north of Mecca, for several weeks' seclusion, prayer and reflection each year. He was deeply troubled by the injustice, discrimination (particularly against women), abuse of power and tribalism he saw all around him.

According to Islamic tradition, it was there that in the year 610, in the month of Ramadan, when he was forty years old, Muhammad was visited one night, while deep in contemplation, by the Angel Gabriel, who revealed to him some words which are now part of the Quran (Quran 53:4–9). At first, he doubted the authenticity of the vision – he believed that it couldn't be real. But, assured by others, and acting on what he had heard and seen, he became an advocate of social and economic justice.

Muhammad's first revelation was followed by others, which continued until his death. He recorded the insights and words he was given, which eventually formed the text of the Quran.

Three years after his first revelation, Muhammad started preaching about what had been revealed to him. His simple, clear-cut message – that God is One, that complete 'surrender' (literally islām) is the only way to discover God – drew huge crowds.

However, his popularity was seen as threatening to the Mecca authorities, and eventually Muhammad found himself driven from the city by its elders. As a result, in 622 he led his followers on a migration (Hijrah) to Medina. This journey was seen as so important that 622 became recognised as the beginning of the Islamic calendar. Within ten years, however, Muhammad had gained so many followers that he was able to return from Medina to conquer Mecca. From here he continued to lead his community until his death in 632.

Some scholars suggest that Muhammad used the term Allah in addressing both pagan Arabs and Jews or Christians in order to establish a common ground for the understanding of the name for God. Says F. E. Peters (Professor Emeritus of Middle Eastern and Islamic Studies and History at New York University): 'The Quran insists, Muslims believe, and historians affirm that Muhammad and his followers worship the same God as the Jews (Quran 29:46). The Quran's Allah is the same Creator God who covenanted with Abraham' (*Islam: A Guide for Jews and Christians*, Princeton University Press, 2003, p. 4).

So we might say that Constantine played as central a role in the development of Islam as a separate religion as he did in the shaping of Christianity three centuries earlier. But unfortunately, because of Constantine, the face of Christianity towards Muhammad was a hostile one, and tragically the face of Islam has often mirrored that same hostility ever since.

10. Abraham Lincoln, the sixteenth US president (1861–65), whose leadership brought about the emancipation of the slaves.
11. Examples of this include Christmas, of which various elements have their origin in pre-Christian festivals that were celebrated around the winter solstice by pagan populations who were later converted to Christianity.

12. From the preface to Vincent J. Donovan, *Christianity Rediscovered* (London: SCM, 1982).
13. For all our concern, there is also progress to celebrate. For instance, Christian–Jewish relationships have undergone a transformation of seismic proportions. In the Middle Ages, popes were engineers of anti-Semitic attitudes. Pope Innocent III's Fourth Lateran Council in 1215, for example, enacted a law whereby Jews living in Christian lands were compelled to wear a badge. The badge was intended to identify Jews as a different and inferior race. It was this move that inspired the long-term, horrific Jewish suffering across Europe which the world has now had much time to grieve over.

Chapter 24: Upside Down and Inside Out

1. Matthew 5:38–48.
2. The early Christians used a wide variety of symbols to express their faith as, at first, they were scared to use the cross publicly, for fear of persecution. The second-century Christian teacher Clement of Alexandria identified a dove, a fish, a ship, a lyre, and an anchor as suitable images to be engraved on Christians' signet-rings (or seals). One of the best-known early Christian symbols, because of its modern revival, is the fish. Early Christians made the Greek word for fish – *ichthus* – into an acronym for 'Jesus Christ, God's Son, Saviour'. However, following the emperor Constantine's conversion to Christianity in the fourth century, crucifixion was abolished as a punishment, and the cross began to be much more publicly promoted as a symbol of Christian faith.

3. 1 John 4:8, 16.
4. A decade ago I wrote a book called *The Lost Message of Jesus*, which contained the following sentences: 'The cross is not a form of cosmic child abuse – a *vengeful* Father, punishing his Son for an offence he did not commit. Rather than a symbol of vengeance or retribution, the cross of Christ is the greatest symbol of love and a demonstration of just how far God the Father and Jesus his Son are prepared to go to prove that love and to bring redemption to their creation.'

   I still stand by that statement. The supporters of what has become known as 'penal substitutionary theory' often represent it as the only valid explanation of the atonement, quoting the writings of various Church Fathers and early Christian writers to bolster their claims. However, as Joel Green and Mark Baker demonstrate in *Rediscovering the Scandal of the Cross*, these conclusions are more easily understood as an anachronistic 'reading back' of modern views onto ancient texts, particularly into the work of Anselm of Canterbury (1033–1109). In fact, penal substitutionary theory rests largely on the work of the nineteenth-century American theologian Charles Hodge who, building on the work of John Calvin's legal mind, argued that a righteous God is angry with sinners and demands justice and that God's wrath could only be appeased through bringing about the violent death of his Son.

   This view of the cross presents us with a God who is first and foremost concerned with retribution for sin that flows from his wrath against sinners. The only way for his anger to be placated is in receiving recompense from those who have wronged him. Although his great love motivates him to send his Son, his wrath remains the driving force behind the need for the cross. God cannot forgive humanity's sin without providing a substitute upon whom his divine wrath can be vented. Only the shedding of blood can nullify his anger. God requires the death of Jesus (as a divine-human representative and substitute for us all) on the cross in order to appease his wrath.

In my view this is built on pre-Christian thought. 'In pagan Greek thought the gods often became angry with men, but their anger could be placated and the good will of the gods obtained by some kind of propitiatory sacrifice', as George Eldon Ladd reminds us in his *Theology of the New Testament*. The emphasis on God's apparent appetite for continuous appeasement through blood sacrifice, present within some Pentateuchal texts, is a reflection of the worship practices of the pagan cults of the nations that surrounded the people of Israel. However, the story of Israel is the story of her journey away from these primal practices towards a new and more enlightened understanding of God. The outcome of this journey of revelation is stated nowhere in the Old Testament more clearly than by the eighth-century-BC prophet Hosea (6:6): 'For I desire mercy, not sacrifice, and acknowledgment of God rather than burnt offerings.'

5. Ernest Hemingway, *A Farewell to Arms* (Scribner, 1929).
6. Tom Wright, *Virtue Reborn* (SPCK, 2010).
7. Matthew 27:46.
8. Psalm 22:22–24.

9. *Come Be My Light: The Private Writings of the Saint of Calcutta*, ed. Brian Kolodiejchuk (Doubleday, 2007).
10. This, of course, is the reason for – as well as the problem with – any form of fundamentalism. It provides the perfect antidote to the need to wrestle with problems and to think. Although it is sometimes argued that fundamentalism is an extreme form of faith, in fact in many ways it represents the opposite of faith. Faith is about questions. Fundamentalism is about certainty. It can only exist in a world of black and white, right and wrong. It cannot tolerate room for doubt – which is why it must always assert not only that it is right but also that all other views are necessarily wrong, wicked and must be silenced.
11. See Matthew 16:24.

Chapter 25: Better Together

1. Adapted and developed from an original idea by St Mary's Church, Maldon.

   Oasis Church Waterloo is the founding part of Oasis Hub Waterloo, which currently consists also of Oasis Johanna Primary School, Oasis South Bank Secondary School, Oasis College of Higher Education, Oasis Community farm, a debt advice centre, a community choir, various football teams, Oasis Hub Café, the Oasis Food Company, Oasis Playspace Children's Centre (and outdoor playspace), and various community partnerships including working with St Thomas', our local hospital, with young people at risk and with all the other churches in the area to deliver the Waterloo Foodbank, which Oasis manages on their behalf.

2. Take Zorro, as another example, who rather than having superhuman powers was simply a very talented swordsman in a mask and a uniform!
3. It is true that although most superheroes work independently, even in their world some choose to work in elite teams – take, for example, The Fantastic Four, The X-Men, Marvel's Avengers and The League of Extraordinary Gentlemen.
4. Michael Riddell, *The Sacred Journey: Reflections on a Life Wholly Lived* (Lion, 2000), 62.
5. Variously attributed to Benjamin Franklin (1706–90), one of the Founding Fathers of the United States, John Ruskin (1819–1900), an influential British art critic, writer, social critic and poet, and others.
6. Genesis 1:27.
7. Hebrews 10:24.
8. The pattern of life-to-life mentoring and learning, of passing on ancient wisdom from generation to generation, from teacher to student, through relationship and example, was at the heart of Hebrew culture and became central to the rabbi's role. Being a student (talmid) of a rabbi was quite different from the experience of a typical twenty-first-century Western student. Today, students are keen to discover what their teacher knows so they can achieve a grade, complete a course or pass an exam. In contrast to this, the student of a rabbi had a very different goal: to imitate their teacher – to become like them. To be a rabbi was to be an inspirational role-model and was a huge responsibility. Rather than being about texts and information, it was primarily about observation, relationship and example.

The Hebrew rabbi's role was dedicated to this bigger task. Their teaching style was, therefore, not primarily about lectures and reading texts, but rather about bringing to their student a whole-life, active learning and mentoring experience. A rabbi's students learnt not just from formal instruction but through imitation and practice. They watched their teacher's every move, noting how they acted and thought in any given situation. Their deepest desire was to follow their rabbi so closely that they would start to think and act and 'do life' in the same way. The rabbinic teaching method of Jesus' day was built around the quality of the relationship between the rabbi and his apprentices as a means of getting to know and understand his way of life.

This rabbi/talmid relationship is famously portrayed in the ancient second-century Hebrew document, the Mishnah, which gives this advice to students: 'you should become dusty in the dust of [your rabbi's] feet; and you should imbibe their words thirstily'. When a rabbi arrived in town, right behind him would be a group of students, doing their best to keep up with him as he walked and taught. After a long day of travelling directly behind their rabbi, the students would be covered in the dust flicked up by his sandals. The more dust, the closer the relationship!

9. The Oasis logo and badge are built around our 'Circle of Inclusion' (our Messy O), which sums up the heart of Oasis and its vision and values.
10. John 8:32.
11. John Donne, *Meditation XVII, Devotions Upon Emergent Occasions.*

12. It is generally agreed that Jesus was multi-lingual and probably spoke at least three languages: Hebrew – the language of the Jewish scriptures; Aramaic – the common language of Judea in the first century AD, which was very closely related to Hebrew; and Greek – the language of the occupying Roman army.
13. *Good Will Hunting* (Miramax Films, 1997).
14. עַדָי (*yada*), meaning 'to know, to see, to perceive, to understand, to know by experience, to have a relationship with'. Jeremiah 22:11–16 explains that 'Josiah [the king] . . . "did what was right and just. . .defended the cause of the poor and needy. . .Is that not what it means to know [*yada*] me?" declares the Lord.' And extending the same sense of 'intimate relationship with' and 'personal experience of' even further, the earthiness of *yada* means that there are about a dozen times when it is even used as a euphemism for knowing someone sexually, as in Genesis 4:1, where the text explains that Adam 'knew Eve his wife'.
15. The definition of the Hebrew word שלום (*shalom*) is 'peace; completeness, nothing missing; nothing broken; well-being'. It occurs more than two hundred and fifty times in the Old Testament. It covers well-being in the widest sense of the word and incorporates notions of contentment, health, prosperity, justice, unity and redemption – at individual, communal, national, international and creational levels – physically, socially, spiritually, educationally, emotionally, economically and environmentally.
16. 'I have come that they may have life, and have it to the full,' says Jesus in John 10:10.
17. If you could travel back in a time capsule and ask the

Hebrews how they found time for their spiritual side in the busyness of life, they would look at you a little confused. Worship was an attitude or approach to the whole of life. There was no divorce or separation between the seemingly mundane and the more formal religious practices. Administration and legislation were part of worship. Tending the soil, caring for the animals, harvesting the crops and sustaining the relationships of the community were acts of thankfulness and worship to God. Every aspect of life was bound up with living in relationship with God, which is why it is natural for the Hebrew scriptures to contain political and social laws relating to the warp and weft of daily life.

Without understanding this context, it is easy to wonder why we have book after book in the Old Testament devoted to what appears to be tedious laws and boring bureaucracy. But the truth is, the Hebrew scriptures were never written with the intention of being either a 'Sunday book' or a devotional manual to provide inspiration in those 'special' moments.

This fundamental notion of a spirituality assimilated into the whole of life is further developed throughout the New Testament. And although the apostle Paul's famous distinction between 'flesh' and 'spirit' has often been seen as being in conflict with this understanding and of implying an absolute separation of the physical from the spiritual, this is to misread him. Paul was a Jew; and his thought is deeply rooted in Hebrew ideas. So, by 'flesh' Paul cannot mean what is physical as opposed to what is invisible: instead, he is referring to all of life (including religion) seen in a narrowly legalistic perspective, whereas by 'spirit' he means all of life (including physical life) seen from the new perspective of following Jesus.

18. Oasis's 'Whole Life Learning' Educational Philosophy – which is the basis of our work around the world – is built upon three ancient Hebrew words and the challenge that flows from them: that of working to ensure that all our students and staff are equipped for life, for strong relationships, for wise decision making and good judgement, which brings well-being and shalom to individuals and whole communities. The three words are:

    Rabbi: my teacher, my guide, a term of respect.
    Yada: to know, to see, to perceive, to understand, to know by experience, to have a relationship with.
    Shalom: peace; completeness; nothing missing; nothing broken; well-being.

19. None of this is to suggest that taking time for practices such as meditation, contemplation and prayer does not have an important place in our development as human beings. We hold certain occasions, events, celebrations and elements to be 'holy' – we believe that in some mysterious way these communicate God's presence.
20. Adapted and developed from a story told by Mike Riddell in *Sacred Journey*, 9.

About Oasis

Being Human is born out of Steve Chalke's experience of working with people and communities around the world through Oasis, the charity that he founded in 1985. A Christian movement that works in eleven countries, Oasis's vision is to transform communities into healthy local neighbourhoods where everyone is included, is able to make a contribution and has the opportunity to reach their God-given potential.

Oasis works in partnership with tens of thousands of people every day in some of the world's most underprivileged neighbourhoods, from slums in India's biggest cities to disadvantaged communities in the UK. In England, as part of this, Oasis is also one of the leading providers of education, serving thousands of primary and secondary school children and their communities on a daily basis. The Oasis mission is the same the world over; to offer integrated, high quality services that benefit the whole person and the whole community – socially, educationally, spiritually, culturally, morally, environmentally, physically, economically and emotionally. So, around the world, Oasis runs schools, youthwork, housing projects, community arts and sports programmes, churches, health centres, adult education, training and employment opportunities, and much more.

2015 marks Oasis' 30th anniversary and this book is testament to the countless people who, inspired by the Oasis vision of community transformation, have served their neighbourhoods over the past three decades.

For further study and discussion resources related to *Being Human*, visit www.oasisuk.org/beinghuman

www.oasisuk.org

@oasis_uk

www.facebook.com/oasisuk